DIVING AND SNORKELING GUIDE TO

The Bahamas
Family Islands
and Grand Bahama
Second Edition

Bob and Charlotte Keller

Pisces Books™
A division of Gulf Publishing Company
Houston, Texas

All photos are by the authors unless otherwise noted.

Cover photo of red-tipped sea goddess, a nudibranch, courtesy of and copyright by Joyce & Frank Burek, 1993.

First edition copyright © 1988 by Bob and Charlotte Keller.

Copyright © 1995 by Gulf Publishing Company, Houston, Texas. All rights reserved. This book, or parts thereof, may not be reproduced in any form without permission of the publisher.

Pisces Books
A division of Gulf Publishing Company
P.O. Box 2608, Houston, Texas 77252-2608

Library of Congress Cataloging-in-Publication Data

Keller, Bob.
    Diving and snorkeling guide to the Bahamas, Family Islands and Grand Bahama / Bob and Charlotte Keller. — 2nd ed.
        p.   cm.
    Includes index.
    ISBN 1-55992-078-5
    1. Skin diving—Bahamas—Guidebooks.   2. Bahamas—Guidebooks. I. Keller, Charlotte.   II. Title.
    GV840.S78K37   1995
    797.2′37296—dc20   94-18171
                                                              CIP

Pisces Books is a trademark of Gulf Publishing Company.

Printed in Hong Kong

10   9   8   7   6   5   4   3   2   1

Table of Contents

How to Use This Guide

This guide is intended to be a companion while you island hop through the Family Islands of the Bahamas. It is impossible to describe all the dive sites that are visited on a regular basis in the 100,000 square miles of ocean of the Bahamas. We have attempted to cover only those areas that are frequently visited by divers, and where services—like dive boats, air fills, and guides—are available.

Some of the islands are rather remote, others are rather rustic, while others are a combination. This is compensated by near-perfect diving.

Divers and snorkelers from all over the world enjoy the colorful flora and fauna abundant in Bahamian waters. Photo courtesy of Bahamas Ministry of Tourism.

Unless you are traveling with your own equipment in the Family Islands, you must rent whatever is needed from one of the dive operators in the area. In many cases there will only be one operator, resort, or hotel on a given island or section of a large island. Therefore, most of the dives mentioned will be dives that are favorites of the operators and will be close-in to shorten boat trips.

There are several great dive sites in these centralized areas, and there are literally thousands of equal or better sites nearby. Because of this, divers have returned year after year to the same area and have been treated to "new" dives on every visit.

The description of the dives in this guide gives you a general overview of the diving a particular area is noted for. Also, it gives you an idea of the conditions on a particular site. This will provide a gauge for photography format and topography, while pointing out special things to look for and serving as a follow-up for log book notations.

Because of the Bahamas' geographic location and the geology of the area, there are really no bad dive areas. Considering this, and the fact that even on a dive vacation most of your time is spent out of the water, we have provided an overview of each island in the Family Islands.

Under the blanket of night, the sticky, flexible arms of a crinoid search the surface of a neighboring sponge for an evening meal.

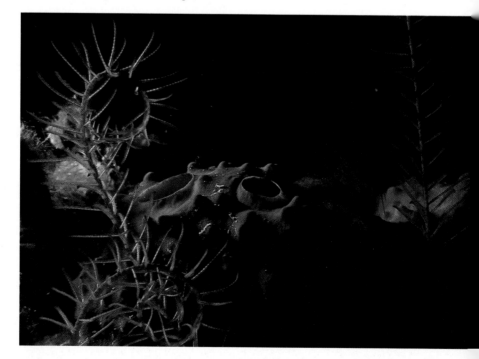

Rating System for Divers and Dive Sites

We have rated each dive according to skill. There are three levels: novice, intermediate, and advanced. A novice diver is considered a recently trained basic diver or a diver who only dives during a dive vacation once a year. An advanced diver is one who has had the additional training of an advanced diver course and is active in diving more than a few times a year. An intermediate diver is between these two divisions.

There are several other factors that are not considered in the rating: physical condition, types of diving the visitor usually does, and personal comfort in a dive situation. These must be judged by the diver himself.

Do not judge your ability on what other people are doing. Only you know your capabilities and limitations. Don't ruin a great vacation attempting to keep up with folks who have more experience.

Many resorts do not require certification but require divers to pass a diver checkout. An increasing number of resorts are using divers' logbooks to determine ability and experience. Without current logbooks, divers are considered novices regardless of their certification levels or claims of experience and may be excluded from certain dives.

Stay within the area of the dive site as outlined by the dive guides or divemasters during the pre-dive briefing. Most dive sites are only a short swim to the edge of a wall with potentially dangerous drop-offs.

Although most divemasters will suggest depths and bottom times, review of the dive tables before a dive should be mandatory. Enjoy this superb diving safely.

The many colors of fish, coral, and plant life can be seen in the glow of the photographer's strobe. It is this predominance of color that makes the coral reefs of the Family Islands a favorite vacation spot for underwater photographers.

1

Overview of the Bahamas

History. In 1992, all America, North and South, celebrated the quincentennial of Columbus' discovery. No one celebrated more than the country of the Bahamas. What most Americans don't know is that Columbus' first landfall in the new world was a small island at the southern end of what we now know as the Bahamas. In a letter he sent to the King of Spain shortly after his discoveries, he wrote, "The shores are embellished with lofty palm trees, whose shade gives a delicious freshness to the air, and the birds and flowers are uncommon and beautiful. I was so delighted with the scene, that I had almost come to the resolutution [sic] of staying here for the remainder of my days; for believe me, Sire, these countries far surpass all the rest of the world in beauty and conveniency." For today's travelers and tourists, Columbus' words are as appropriate now as they were five hundred years ago.

Soon after his arrival, Columbus and his followers enslaved all the Lucayan Indians, who then inhabited the area, and shipped them off to Hispaniola to mine gold. The entire Lucayan race was soon extinct.

Following Columbus' discovery, the Bahamas were explored extensively by Ponce de León. Ponce de León was with Columbus on his second journey to the new world, and he returned with his own ships in 1513, searching for the fountain of youth. F. de Herrera, one of Ponce de León's crew, named the area *Bajamar,* the Spanish word for shallow water. The water was so clear that even where it was deep, it seemed shallow. In his travels, Ponce de León recorded landing on most of the major islands in the Bahamas.

Ideally located, the Bahamas straddle the Tropic of Cancer and set alongside the Gulf Stream, both of which help to create near-perfect weather. With an average winter temperature of 72° and a summer average, kept moderate by the trade winds, of 82°, the island country of the Bahamas is the perfect destination for travelers seeking to visit a place where the fountain of youth would seem unnecessary. It won't be long after arrival before your watch starts running on Bahamian time, which seems to follow no conventional time zone, and your mind begins to fall into step.

Today, that clear water described by F. de Herrera has become a mecca for divers from around the world. Every year, the Bahamas hosts millions of visitors. Many of them aren't divers, but it is estimated that more non-divers take up diving or snorkeling for the first time after a visit to the Bahamas than to any other place in the world.

4

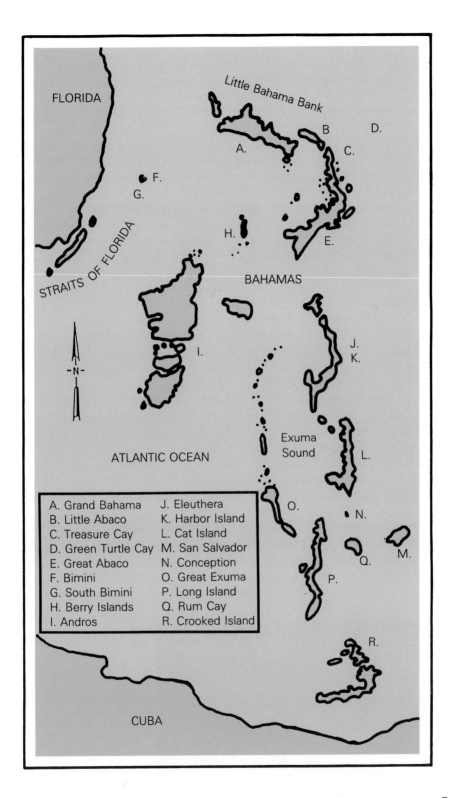

FLORIDA

Little Bahama Bank

A. Grand Bahama
B. Little Abaco
C. Treasure Cay
D. Green Turtle Cay
E. Great Abaco
F. Bimini
G. South Bimini
H. Berry Islands
I. Andros
J. Eleuthera
K. Harbor Island
L. Cat Island
M. San Salvador
N. Conception
O. Great Exuma
P. Long Island
Q. Rum Cay
R. Crooked Island

STRAITS OF FLORIDA

BAHAMAS

-N-

ATLANTIC OCEAN

Exuma Sound

CUBA

Usually described as seven hundred islands, the 5,353 square miles of land mass, spread over 100,000 square miles of Atlantic Ocean, is actually 29 islands, 661 cays, and 2,390 rocks that rise permanently above the water line.

Most of the population is centered in Nassau (New Providence Island), the capital city. Of the 251,000 population, 59% live in Nassau; the rest live on what are referred to by Bahamians as the Family Islands. Formally referred to as the out islands, the government decreed that reference to the islands, except for New Providence (Nassau) and Grand Bahama (Freeport), should be "Family Islands," to join the commonwealth of the Bahamas together as one large family. Many natives believe it is so named because the workers are all in Nassau and Freeport and their families are on the other islands.

The first census in the Bahamas was taken in 1671 and showed a population of 1,097 inhabitants; of these, 433 were slaves. In the late 1700s, when American revolutionists started talking about independence from England, many colonists who were loyal to the crown and believed the rumors that independence would put an end to slavery moved entire plantations, including slaves, to the Bahamas. Not finding the lush soil conditions they had left behind in the Carolinas and having exhausted their funds, many returned, leaving their slaves behind. England and the Bahamas passed legislation in 1833, a full generation before America did, outlawing the owning of slaves. Today the population of the Bahamas is 85% black.

The Bahamas were under British jurisdiction for more than three hundred years, and English has always been the official language of the islands. In 1964, self-government was granted, and full independence was attained within the Commonwealth on July 10, 1973.

The larger inhabited Family Islands are served by Bahamasair Airlines, the official airline of the Bahamas, and many islands are served on a regular basis by charter airline companies. All the inhabited islands are served by mail boats under contract with the government. The mail boats do provide economical passenger service, but service is slow and often not on schedule.

When the Indians greeted Columbus with gifts of wild parrots and orchids that grew in this tropic paradise, he was so amazed at the lifestyle of this remote island nation that he brought back to Spain not only some of the Indians but several of their customs. The Indians were sleeping in rope swings hung

Historic Harbor Island displays classic examples of early Bahamas history. Unscathed by hurricanes, these houses date back to the eighteenth century.

Orchids are the wildflowers of the "Bush" on most of the Family Islands. These hearty air plants thrive in the tropic weather of the Bahamas.

between trees; they called the swings hamacas. After Columbus' return, these cotton nets became standard bunks for sailors traveling the high seas.

Columbus also brought back maize, potatoes, tobacco, and avocados. He also learned and brought back the words, "cannibal," "buccaneer," "canoe," and "hurricane," among others.

This island nation now boasts tourism as its major industry. With that boast comes the promise that tourists will be treated as Columbus was, with open arms and stylish grace.

Customs. With tourism as the Bahamas' main industry and the Bahamas' proximity to the United States, customs and immigration restrictions are minimal.

Underwater plants, colorful fish, and intricate coral transform the ocean bottom into a literal garden of visual delights.

Proof of citizenship and a return ticket are required before you enter the Bahamas. A passport, birth certificate, or voter registration card are accepted as proof of citizenship. Driver's licenses are not.

A Bahamas immigration card must be filled out and presented to immigration at the port of entry. This will be furnished by the airline or charter service during your flight. If your destination does not have customs officers, the plane will stop at a point-of-entry airport and all passengers and luggage will have to be cleared before landing at the final destination.

Bahamian customs is tourist-oriented and will do everything possible to clear you quickly and courteously. No firearms or drugs are allowed, so be sure any prescription medication is clearly marked in its original container with the prescription affixed to the container.

There is a departure tax of $15.00 per person, payable when surrendering your embarkation card. If you want your passport stamped by Bahamian Customs, you must ask a customs officer.

U.S. customs has established a United States point-of-entry check station in Nassau to accommodate travelers leaving the country through that city by scheduled airlines. Charter flight travelers will still have to clear customs when they arrive in the United States.

Transportation. Transportation to the islands is usually available through the resorts that serve the individual islands. Bahamasair Airlines and several charter companies serve the major islands on a regular schedule. Flights are convenient from Miami and Ft. Lauderdale, direct to the various islands, via charter service. Bahamasair Airlines only serves the Family Islands via Nassau. Nassau can be reached directly by commercial carriers from many U.S. and European cities.

Transportation on the islands will certainly be part of the vacation memory. Taxis are ready to serve airport arrivals with "trans," as it's called, to the various resorts. Drivers must be licensed to drive in the Bahamas. Drivers licensed to drive in the Family Islands must qualify for an additional license to drive on the streets of Nassau. On remote islands where there are few roads and minimal taxis, the resorts will meet the plane and provide transportation to your lodging. Taxi rates from the airport to the resort or hotel are usually a fixed amount.

After the spring rains, white lilies cover the sand dunes along the shore. These plants, as hardy as they are beautiful, help to stabilize the shifting sands of the dunes.

Most resorts can arrange a rental car if you want to take a day off from diving and tour the island alone. Don't expect a car similar to one back home. These arrangements are usually a private deal with one of the local car owners who can spare his "trans" for a day.

Although most cars are American and have the steering wheel on the left, if you do go driving on your own, remember the rule in the Bahamas is to drive on the left. Tourists with current driver's licenses need not acquire a Bahamian license to drive here.

The roads in the Family Islands are much better than would be expected, but be prepared. Unlike fishing trips where one always arrives the week *after* the fishing was great, expect to arrive the week *before* the road repair is scheduled.

If your plans are to spend a week or two at one resort on one island, the resort management can usually arrange an over-and-back charter for a day in Nassau, if desired.

Hotels and Resorts. Hotels on the Family Islands usually involve a resort arrangement, providing rooms, meals, diving, and entertainment. Quoted room rates usually include meals and amenities. Entertainment and activities are offered at little or no cost, and sometimes free snorkeling or scuba instruction is available.

Dress and atmosphere is casual. Swimsuits are the accepted attire even in the dining rooms during the day. Many Family Island resorts have a "no tie" rule.

Dining. For the most part, meals are arranged by the resort as part of a package, but all the islands offer a variety of restaurants for a change of pace. The restaurants offer American and European cuisine for the convenience of tourists, but if the opportunity arises, be sure to try Bahamian food.

Many resorts set aside one evening as Bahamian night and feature all Bahamian dishes, including crabs, bread pudding, and various conch (pronounced "konk") entrees.

An underwater garden of gorgonians—soft corals—bend and blow in the breeze of the ocean current. Like the hard corals, they are actually colonies of millions of animals joined together to form a seemingly single "plant."

Fresh fish is exactly that. Bahamian fishing boats have a "live" well and fish are kept alive until purchased by the customer. Lobster is native to the Bahamas and is a staple on most menus. Wait until you try lobster on the barbecue!

Pineapples are a native product. Smaller and therefore less commercially marketable, these "pines" are much sweeter than the Hawaiian variety.

Tipping. Tipping for services rendered is the same as in the United States, about 10 to 15 percent. Some restaurants add a tip to the bill before it is presented. Any additional gratuity is up to the customer.

Some resorts offer package deals that include room, meals, diving, and gratuity for one price. The gratuity, a percentage of the total bill, is then extracted and paid to the employees based upon an agreement with the management. In some cases this means the yard sweeper gets the same share as the divemaster or bartender. If staff members have excelled, it is acceptable to provide an additional gratuity.

Currency. Since Bahamian currency always equals the dollar in value, American money is accepted and change given in U.S. money. Bahamian currency is very colorful with hidden imprints of shells and dignitaries in the paper money. Paper money and coin denominations are the same as U.S. currency with two exceptions—Bahamian money has a paper fifty-cent bill and a three-dollar bill. These are popular tourist souvenirs, therefore, they are not common.

Family Island banking is true "branch" banking in most cases. Banks are branches of larger institutions in Nassau and bank personnel are flown to the branch only one or two days a week. If you need to bank during your stay, it is best to do it when passing through Nassau on the way to the Family Islands, or contact the resort or hotel ahead of time and find out when the local bank is open.

Most stores, restaurants, resorts, and hotels accept credit cards, but it is best to check in advance because it is not uncommon for only one card to be accepted. Most establishments will not accept personal checks drawn on banks in the United States. Travelers' checks are accepted almost everywhere.

Shopping. Few consumer goods are produced in the Bahamas. Family Island residents travel to Nassau for major purchases or use mail order. As a result, stores outside the big cities carry only staples and a few imported articles.

You will find hand-woven straw or raffia items and locally produced fabrics and clothes. No matter how small the island, you will always find a "straw market," even though it may be one room of a local house. If you don't see what you want, ask the owner and someone will make it for you, probably while you wait.

Fine fabrics and garments made in the Bahamas are usually available at a local boutique, either in the resort or the nearby village. The Bahamas' hand-batiked *Androsia* garments are high quality and reasonably priced.

Shopping can be a fun adventure in the Family Islands; but if you're likely to contract "mall withdrawal," the Family Islands are not for you.

Electricity. Electricity in the Bahamas is the same as in the United States, 110 volts and 60-cycle, and the wall outlets are the same, so no adapters are needed. Most remote island resorts generate their own electricity. This can sometimes be hazardous to sensitive electric or electronic equipment. A surge protector would be a handy item to add to your luggage. If you have a rechargeable strobe or video battery pack, the chargers cannot withstand high voltage surges—a common problem under these conditions. Also, you might want to add a small flashlight to your luggage.

Drinking Water. Fresh water is a precious commodity. Artesian wells and some cisterns are the primary source of fresh water. On some remote islands this water is more salt than fresh, so fresh water must be distilled locally.

Several islands have an abundance of fresh water. Andros, for example, has enough excess water that bargeloads are shipped daily to Nassau to augment the supply on New Providence Island.

Even the freshest of water, however, is probably more salty than most Americans are accustomed to. Persons on a low-salt or no-salt diet should consider this.

A tiny hermit crab looks into the mouth of disaster as a sea star anticipates an easy meal.

2

Diving in the Bahamas

Geology. The geological makeup of each of the islands in the Bahamas archipelago is generally the same. As a result, there is great similarity in dive sites from island to island. Most of the underwater formations are made of limestone as a result of old and new coral build-up, rather than volcanic outpouring.

Millions of years ago, when the oceans were deeper, coral built up to the surface as it still does today. During the Ice Age, water was drawn to the poles forming the ice cap, the depth of the oceans dropped, and the coral was exposed to the elements. These coral/limestone mountains, left exposed to the effects of wind and rain over thousands of years, formed crevices and valleys. Today, these irregular areas are submerged and covered with new coral growth. They formed the foundation for the classic dive sites the Bahamas are famous for. The face of these former mountains form an underwater wall around most of the islands providing another unique dive potential—wall diving.

Similar to a million hungry mouths, the coral polyps open in the dark to feed on passing plankton. During the day, these tentacles stay housed in the stony case of the coral.

The spectacular visibility of Bahamian waters is guaranteed—there are no rivers flowing into the sea to cloud it and the Gulf Stream provides a constant flow purifying it.

Due to a consistent geological makeup, most of the islands provide a shallow reef at the 10–15-foot (3–5-meter) level with shallow-depth coral and animal life. Also, a reef is at the 50-foot (15-meter) depth, with its comparable life. An additional reef at 80–90 feet (24–27 meters) is also present, before dropping off to great depths, sometimes as deep as 6,000 feet (1,829 meters).

With the myriad coral structures surrounding the 2,400-plus islands and cays, there are endless dive sites available to divers. Most dive sites are exclusive to particular resorts or dive operators who serve a certain area. Most, if not all, of your diving in the Bahamas will be with one of these operators or resorts. The dive sites listed in this guide are either old favorites, or current favorites of the resort or operator serving a particular area. Since these operators take pride in their sites, they will "rest" a site from time to time to allow the coral and fish to replenish. If a dive operation is not diving one of the listed sites in this guide when you visit, you can be assured their alternate dive site will be as good or better.

Boat Diving. Because of the reef locations, boat diving with dive guides will be the rule for the major sites and all the sites listed in this guide. Some beach diving is available on select islands, but this is the exception and will be in very shallow water.

Photo opportunities abound among the gracefully spreading arms of gorgonians anchored on the walls of drop-offs. Photo: Randi Kent.

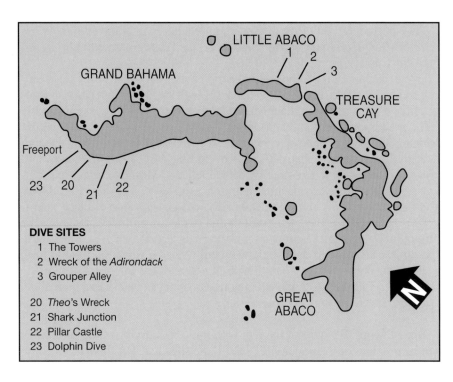

DIVE SITES
1 The Towers
2 Wreck of the *Adirondack*
3 Grouper Alley

20 *Theo*'s Wreck
21 Shark Junction
22 Pillar Castle
23 Dolphin Dive

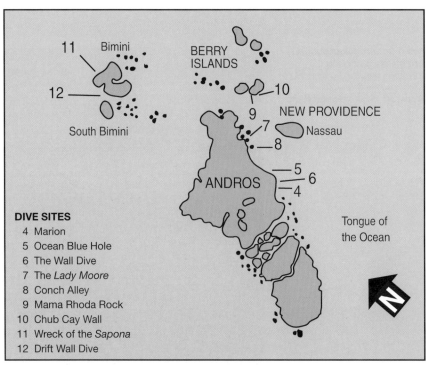

DIVE SITES
4 Marion
5 Ocean Blue Hole
6 The Wall Dive
7 The *Lady Moore*
8 Conch Alley
9 Mama Rhoda Rock
10 Chub Cay Wall
11 Wreck of the *Sapona*
12 Drift Wall Dive

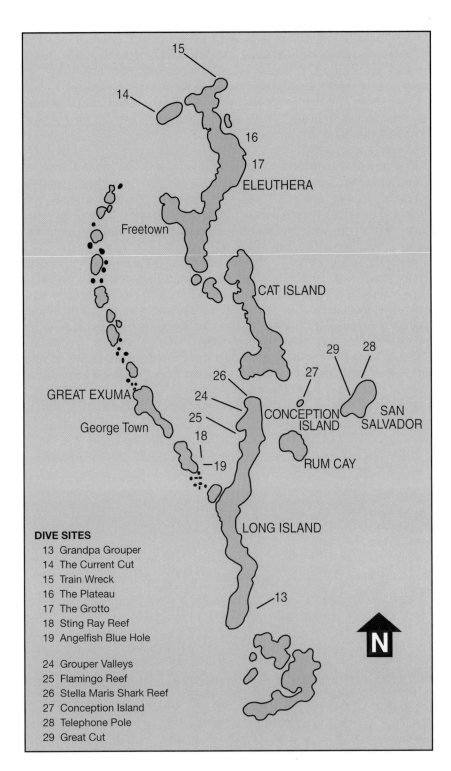

15

14

16

17

ELEUTHERA

Freetown

CAT ISLAND

29   28

26   27

24

GREAT EXUMA

25   CONCEPTION   SAN
ISLAND   SALVADOR

18

George Town

19

RUM CAY

LONG ISLAND

DIVE SITES
13 Grandpa Grouper
14 The Current Cut
15 Train Wreck
16 The Plateau
17 The Grotto
18 Sting Ray Reef
19 Angelfish Blue Hole

24 Grouper Valleys
25 Flamingo Reef
26 Stella Maris Shark Reef
27 Conception Island
28 Telephone Pole
29 Great Cut

13

N

Most of the dive boats are open-deck pontoon boats. Even on the islands with eastern exposure to the open ocean, these are more than adequate for the seas surrounding the dive sites. At some resorts these boats have bars, heads, and changing rooms that double as darkrooms if needed.

Some resorts make boats available to guests on a rental basis, but unless you want to dive the same site over and over, diving with the operators and the dive guides is the best route.

Equipment. All the dive operations provide tanks and weights in the cost of the dive. Some have scuba equipment for rent. Dive qualification requirements vary: some require certification, some require current log books, while others require that you pass a diver check-out with one of their divemasters. Check-out usually consists of mask clearing, buddy breathing, and proper ascent procedures.

Wet suits are not needed for thermal protection but are useful for protection against sharp coral. Diving in a lightweight wet suit is sufficient. An old pair of pants may be substituted for a wet suit. Gloves are recommended for protection against sharp coral. Many dive sites are populated with friendly grouper and yellowtail snapper that are fed regularly by the guides. Gloves are a good precaution when feeding fish.

Check with the resort or dive operation for the availability of rental photo equipment and photo supplies and services. If it is not available at a specific resort, it is probably not available on the island. It is a good idea to bring what you need and not depend upon availability at the resort.

From the air, visiting divers get their introduction to the Tongue of the Ocean and the renowned walls of the Bahamas.

Certification. Most of the divemasters and guides are certified instructors; however, certification classes are the exception rather than the rule. Most dive operations provide "resort courses" that will enable you to dive with them but do not provide full certification.

Marine Life. The same types of marine life will be found from island to island. Some areas have an abundance of a certain type while others are famous for a proliferation of a particular species. On most of the Family Islands, the Bahamian government has designated areas as protected underwater parks. Nothing may be removed from these areas. This often includes "dead" shells, since other animals often use these discarded shells for residences. Guides will provide information about local rules on hunting and gathering which vary from island to island. Check with your destination operators before arriving to verify specific diving activities.

Night Diving. Some operations schedule night diving on a regular basis or as part of a package. Others conduct night dives when several guests are interested. Most operations provide lights if they have night dives, or divers may use their own dive lights.

Between reef and surface even novice divers and snorkelers can enjoy the unique experience of looking up at fish, a privilege shared only by those who venture beneath the sea.

17

3

Diving the Abaco Islands

Located in the far northeast section of the country, the Abacos are a dog-leg stretch of islands and cays more than 130 miles long, from Walker's Cay in the north to Hole in the Wall to the south. The Abacos are perhaps the most unique of any group of islands in the country. There are two main islands, Great Abaco and Little Abaco, and too many cays to count. Abacos are bordered by the open Atlantic on the east and the Little Bahamas Bank on the west.

Ponce de León passed Elbow Cay on Easter Sunday in 1513 and stopped at what is now known as Sandy Cay. He named the cay La Vieja after the woman who lived there and was believed to be the last native inhabitant of the Bahamas.

Today, Marsh Harbour on Great Abaco is the third largest city in the Bahamas. Abaco, consisting of Great and Little Abaco, is the second largest island mass in the Bahamas.

The red and white striped lighthouse at Hope Town on Elbow Cay is one of the most photographed lighthouses in the world. The Abaco chain claims several other titles, including boat building capital of the Bahamas and sailing capital of the world. On Walker's Cay is the largest tropical fish farm in the world.

Lumbering is a major industry. Unlike other islands which were once covered with valuable lumber, Abaco's forests have been maintained and reforested to keep the industry alive. Sustaining the forests has preserved the parrot population on the island. It has also provided material for boat building, a skill renowned on Man-O-War Cay and other cays.

The Towers 1

Typical Depth Range:	60 feet (18 meters)
Typical Current Conditions:	Slight to none
Expertise Required:	Novice
Access:	Boat

The base of the coral formations called the Towers will register 60 feet (18 meters) on your depth gauge. At low tide, the tops will stick out of the water. The size of the formations and the depth of the water represent the major different depths that support all types of coral. If a diver were to start at the surface and swim in a corkscrew-shaped path down the formations, almost every species of coral could be viewed.

Because the variety of depth is all in one spot, and all the food chain is together, the animal life on this site is as varied as anywhere. This dive is a popular night dive site.

At the top, all the shallow reef species thrive, and deeper, the larger fish abound. Don't be surprised to see large tarpon cruise by in pairs, and almost always a flight of eagle rays will circle the Towers on a scouting mission. And watch for eyes as you circle the Towers to the bottom—many eels, lobsters, and crabs call this site home.

◀ ▲ *At rest during daylight hours, Caribbean star coral polyps remain closed within their exoskeletal formation. After dusk, the polyps open and stand ready to grab drifting zooplankton that rise from the depths during the night.*

Typical Depth Range:	25 feet (8 meters)
Typical Current Conditions:	None
Expertise Required:	Novice and above
Access:	Boat

This dive is a certified wreck dive. It's not the popular recently sunk ship sitting neatly on the bottom with doorways to swim in and out of, but a true wreck of treasure hunter fame. The *Adirondack* was a wooden Union gun ship sunk during the Civil War.

It was a 60-foot (18-meter) gun runner, and amongst some of the debris two 11-foot (3-meter) bore cannons can be found. The old capstan is still visible.

The hard pan bottom sports a few small coral heads, but there are lots of sea fans around. All the sea fans provide home for many flamingo tongue shells. All the reef fish are present, and you'll almost always see a lobster or two. This is a super dive for new divers yet still exciting for the old salts.

A school of juvenile reef fish seem to serve as sentries for the Bahamian lobster crouched beneath a shallow ledge. Though lobster is a staple in the Bahamas, conservation of the species is maintained by a closed season during the mating period.

Grouper Alley 3

Typical Depth Range:	40 Feet (12 meters)
Typical Current Conditions:	None
Expertise Required:	Novice
Access:	Boat

    This site is typical Bahamian dive country: a sandy bottom with large coral heads that reach to within ten feet of the surface. Filled with a variety of coral and all the reef fish that frequent this type area, it's a photographer's dream and perfect for someone who just wants a walk, make that a swim, in an underwater garden. Never mind that the life is all animal and not vegetable—it still computes in the mind as a garden.

    This site abounds in large fish and other sea creatures. Turtles and sharks are common, as are eels and a variety of rays. A few caverns on the coral heads are big enough to explore without danger.

    Named for the abundance of groupers in the area, the real treat on this dive site is one of it's famous long-time inhabitants: A barracuda named Gilly has called this area home for almost ten years, and welcomes divers and gladly poses for photos. He appears to love the divers.

    One picture of Gilly appeared on the cover of *Skin Diver* magazine a few years back, so don't be surprised if he acts like a superstar—he is.

The barracuda, whose teeth show even when his mouth is closed, is ominous to say the least. Seen throughout the Bahamas, this reef inhabitant watches and waits. Seldom known to bother divers, the barracuda is fast and will strike at shiny objects.

In some areas, one type of coral dominates the "landscape." Here, a variety of stony corals overlap and intertwine against a backdrop of blue.

Coral

More than a thousand species of coral have been identified as the builders of the living reef that makes up the background of all the tropical dive sites in the world. The different species of life known as coral polyps are actually carnivorous animals. They prey upon the small plankton that are invisible to the naked eye.

They are exoskelotal, meaning their hard protective body tissue is on the outside. This hard mass, the limestone that is the basis for all the coral reefs, is left behind when the animals die; new colonies are built upon the old.

Some of the islands in the Bahamas are estimated to be 20,000-foot-thick layers (6,096 meters) of built-up coral. Considering some coral polyps grow only one-half inch (1.27 centimeters) per year, divers must be careful not to damage the coral reefs.

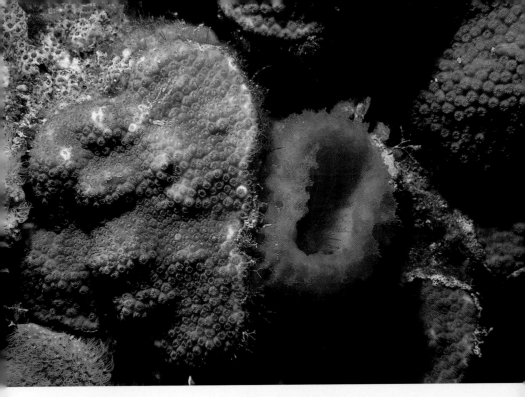

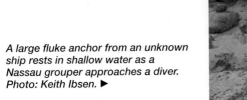
▲ A small shrimp is nestled in the basket sponge, demonstrating the symbiosis that exists among the various creatures on the sea floor. There is one variety of sponge that in a similar situation permanently closes its opening, making the shrimp a prisoner. The sponge then provides food for the shrimp for the rest of the shrimp's life.

A large fluke anchor from an unknown ship rests in shallow water as a Nassau grouper approaches a diver. Photo: Keith Ibsen. ▶

4

Diving Andros

One of the first Bahamian islands inhabited, Andros is perhaps the least explored. Underwater, along Andros' eastern shore, the second largest barrier reef in the world may also be the least explored in terms of diving sites. Nevertheless, the hundreds of charted and named dive sites that have been explored are sure to meet with diver approval.

"The Sleeping Giant" as Bahamians call it, Andros Island is the largest of the 700 islands that comprise the nation of the Bahamas. Andros is just over 100 miles (161 kilometers) long and 40 miles (64 kilometers) wide. Along the western edge, the shallow "Bahamas Banks" were once rich with sponges until a parasite killed them off in the late 1930s. Ninety percent of the sponges were wiped out, and the sponge industry died.

Along the eastern shore, where all the inhabitants live, the island borders the Tongue of the Ocean. This trench running the length of the island drops off to depths of 6,000 feet (1,829 meters). A U.S. Navy base near Fresh Creek uses the trench's depth as a testing area for submarines.

Andros is a collection of islands referred to as one. The southern part of the island is less inhabited and one of the few nesting places for the pink flamingos that are the national bird of the Bahamas. All the dive operations and resort hotels are in the central and northern part of the island.

Andros is only 25 miles (40 kilometers) from Nassau and supplies most of Nassau's water. Water is shipped daily on barges from ports at the northern part of the island. Nickolstown, at the northern end of the island, is set to shortly host cruise ships that tour the islands.

Another product of Andros is *Androsia,* a hand-batiked cloth that is manufactured in Fresh Creek in central Andros. It is fast becoming the fabric of the Bahamas. Colorful Androsia garments can be found in boutiques throughout the islands.

Andros is famous for its various woods and the Androsians who use it to build winning boats for the Family Island Regatta held each year off Georgetown in the Exumas.

At one time the island was covered with trees. About 30 years ago, all the "Andros pines," which yield a very hard and colorful wood, were harvested by American lumber companies. Cutting the trees is said to have destroyed the nesting places of the infamous *chickcharnies.* These Androsian elves, who are believed to live in high trees, are three-fingered, pointed-bearded, red-eyed creatures who have the same kind of legendary reputation as Irish leprechauns. Keep an eye out! You never know what your luck might be.

◀ *The Caserina, or Australian, pine is common on the islands. It offers shade and beauty, but watch out for its sticky, sharp cones beneath your bare feet.*

Typical Depth Range:	70 feet (21 meters)
Typical Current Conditions:	None
Expertise Required:	Intermediate
Access:	Boat

The Marion is a mobile construction crane which was placed on a barge to do offshore construction for the U.S. Navy.

The Marion was destroyed when the barge capsized. A larger crane lifted the Marion and the barge, and relocated them to their present location.

The barge still contains the tools and spare parts for the crane. It lies upside down across two giant coral heads. The crane rests alongside it, with the tracks a few feet away from the main body.

The floor around the area is flat sand, dotted with coral heads. All the reef fish that would normally be present are now joined by thousands of fish that seem to search for wrecks as new homes.

With good visibility, this is the perfect background setting for unusual underwater model photography.

A school of grunts flows with the surge. These fish are so named because of the grunting sound that can be heard underwater by divers.

Ocean Blue Hole

Typical Depth Range:	50–100 feet (15–30 meters)
Typical Current Conditions:	None
Expertise Required:	Intermediate
Access:	Boat

Jacques Cousteau and the crew of *Calypso* came to Andros Island several years ago to study the famous ocean blue holes that surround Andros, the largest of the Bahamian islands. There were no significant discoveries made by his study; blue holes are as much a mystery today as they have always been.

Pedersen shrimp man a cleaning station. Large fish stop at the cleaner stations, open their mouths and gills, and allow the shrimp and smaller cleaner fish to remove parasites that can't be scrubbed by rubbing—the fish's own method of cleaning itself.

Large sink holes located offshore are connected to the parent island by a labyrinth of tunnels. Since some of the tunnels reach unknown depths, this only compounds the mystery of these offshore pits on the ocean bottom. They are deeper than the surrounding area, and appear a richer blue when viewed from the air, hence the name "blue holes." Some are smaller in diameter, and cause a strong flushing effect throughout the network of tunnels dependent upon the changing tide.

There is one hole located a mile off the shore of central Andros that is unaffected by tide changes. This blue hole is approximately 300 feet (90 meters) across and about 45 feet (14 meters) in depth, then drops another 50 to 60 feet (15 to 18 meters) to the bottom of the hole. The bottom appears to have fallen in one drop creating a plug in the hole's center. Surrounding the plug is a circular ring about 15 feet (5 meters) in diameter that drops to unknown depths. Researchers have gone as far down as 200 feet (60 meters) with the bottom still out of sight.

About 10 feet (3 meters) below the rim at about the 60-foot (18-meter) level, a therocline lowers the water temperature about 10°F. This slight change to cooler water is refreshing. The areas surrounding the rim and the bottom of the hole are dotted with small coral heads and many "cleaner" fish as well as reef fish.

The best part of this dive is the swim through the cavern area between the bottom of the hole and the wall. Sheared cliffs are located on both sides. There are countless tunnels leading off to nowhere and an endless abyss below.

This dive is safe when conducted with at least two divemasters from the local resort. There is little silt to kick up, therefore, the last or slowest diver sees as much as the first. The main part of the dive is at the 100-foot (30-meter) level, so caution must be taken to follow the instructions of the guides regarding time and depth.

A diver glides behind a black coral bush that grows on the wall in 80 feet (24 meters) of water. At this depth, the warm colors are lost and the coral stalks appear black with deep green fronds. The hard skeleton is black, but in light the coral is actually a red-orange hue. ▶

The Wall Dive 6

Typical Depth Range:	80–185 feet (24–56 meters)
Typical Current Conditions:	None
Expertise Required:	Advanced or above
Access:	Boat

About a mile and a half (2.4 kilometers) off the eastern shore of Andros, the edge of the coral shelf drops down radically to 6,000 feet (1,829 meters). This deep trench, running the length of the island, is known as the Tongue of the Ocean. It was here, over two decades ago, that wall diving as we know it today began.

The dive has two options. Divers qualified for a deep dive may go to the 185-foot (56-meter) level, and those less qualified, or choosing not to go that deep, stay at 80 feet (24 meters) on the reef at the top of the wall.

On the deep portion, divers swim over the edge and glide down to the 185-foot (56-meter) level, where there is a shelf running the length of the wall. The shoreline was here millions of years ago during the Ice Age, but now it is a layer of shelves and cave-like impressions.

Divers are allowed just a few minutes' stop at this level and then return to the 80-foot (24-meter) edge for the continuance of the dive.

At that depth, divers can expect a feeling of euphoria caused by the excess nitrogen in their systems. This passes when coming back above the 100-foot (30-meter) level. This dive is always made with enough dive guides to oversee all guests and each other.

Dropping to that depth, between the wall and the rich blue of deep water, is truly inspiring. Uncut black coral bushes as large as Christmas trees dot the crevices as you descend. Occasionally, large pelagic fish, including marlins, sailfish, sharks, and giant sunfish, can be seen in the distance.

Caution: This dive should only be made accompanied by experienced dive guides. Each diver should be aware of his depth and bottom time as indicated by the guides and keep his own depth and time records. As this dive is planned, there is no decompression required, but hanging off at 10 feet (3 meters) for five minutes is always recommended after being below shallow-water dive depths.

Small Hope Bay Lodge has been conducting this dive for almost thirty years without incident. Dick Birch, the founder and still owner of Small Hope, started wall diving when he moved here from Canada in 1960. Since that time, thousands have safely shared in the beauty of this deep dive.

The Christmas tree worm's tentacles gather nutrients from the surrounding water. If you get too close, it will quickly retreat into its tube. ▶

Wall Diving

Because of the geologic makeup of many of the islands in the Bahamas, there are shear walls that drop to great depths a relatively short distance offshore. These drop-offs have spawned a specific type of diving called wall diving.

Some wall dives approach a depth of almost 200 feet (61 meters) and therefore are of very short duration. The resorts or dive operators who provide these dives are keenly aware of the expertise required and the potential dangers involved, and therefore allow only divers who are physically and mentally qualified to make the dives. Beyond the 100-foot (30-meter) mark, a diver is likely to experience *nitrogen narcosis.*

Nitrogen narcosis is a euphoric state, usually harmless, that can lead to problems in an uncontrolled situation.

The dive resorts and dive operations who offer deep diving are aware of this and have excellent safeguards when dealing with divers under these conditions. Divers must have some diving experience with the resort or operator before they are allowed to experience these dives. The final decision still rests with the diver. If you are unsure, it is best to miss a dive or opt for the shallow dive offered that day.

Typical Depth Range:	40–80 feet (12–24 meters)
Typical Current Conditions:	None
Expertise Required:	Novice
Access:	Boat

The *Lady Moore,* though a new wreck dive, will soon be on the rolls of "must dive" wrecks in the Bahamas. An all steel mail boat, the *Lady Moore* sits upright on the bottom in an area of low coral. Divers can, at different points, swim under the hull in natural channels cut through the coral.

The short 15-minute boat ride to this dive site has made it one of the popular dives on North Andros. The *Lady Moore* has only been on the bottom since May of 1990, but the local fish began calling it home right away.

Schools of horse-eye jacks and barracudas can be seen on almost every dive. And the surrounding low coral provides a perfect photo setting for the Atlantic spadefish that frequent the area.

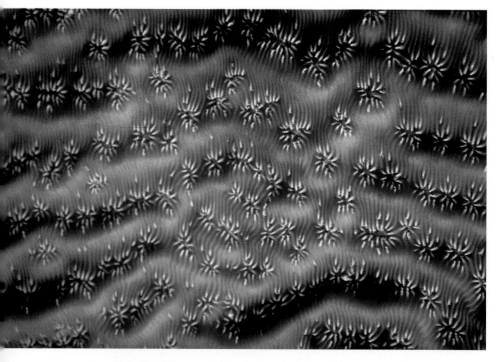

Like the glittering fabric of an evening gown, the surface of Caribbean platter coral is covered with "stars" which are actually the mouths of individual animals that provide part of the fabric that is the coral reefs of the Bahamas.

Conch Alley

Typical Depth Range:	35–55 feet (11–17 meters)
Typical Current Conditions:	None
Expertise Required:	Novice
Access:	Boat

Conch (pronounced konk) is the national food of the Bahamas. The queen conch, growing to full size in three years, has one of the most beautiful shells in the world. Perhaps that's why the official name for those who study shells is conchologists.

The queen conch usually feeds and grazes in the underwater grass flats. These areas are very plain compared to the colorful sculptured reefs for which Bahamas diving is famous. As a result, divers see endless conch shells used to landscape the various islands and enjoy the multitude of dishes made from the meat, but never get to see the animal, with its tentacle-like eyes, in its natural habitat.

This dive site is the exception. The area is covered with soft and hard coral, all the Bahamian reef fish seen on other sites, and the queen conch on its home ground.

A new treat has been added to this dive since the first edition of this guide. Now, schools of gray angels are fed by divers. There are never less than 20 in a school, and three special "angels," nicknamed the Three Stooges, will last in the memory of every diver who visits here. Feeding the parrotfish is also something unique that this dive provides. There are large ledges under which nurse sharks can often be seen sleeping during the day. In those same crevices, crabs and lobsters abound as do feather worms and nudibranchs. This is an excellent dive site for macro and close-up photography.

A diver inspects a Queen Conch, which is unrivaled as a local delicacy. Conches are often found on sandy bottoms and in shallow eel grass beds where they feed on algae. Photo: Keith Ibsen.

5

Diving the Berry Islands

Perched on the edge of the 6,000-foot-deep (1,829 meters) Tongue of the Ocean, the 30 or so cays that make up the Berry Islands were for years a secret known only to the wealthy. Nineteen miles east of Bimini, one of the best kept secrets was that its fishing was as good as Bimini's. A better kept secret was its fine diving sites.

One of the stops on Ponce de León's first voyage in 1513 in his search for the Fountain of Youth, this group of islands was almost unheard of until 1813 when a colony was set up for freed slaves. Part of that original colony still exists on Whale Cay.

In the 1930s, some of the islands were developed and sold to individuals. Several of the islands are still privately owned.

Thirty-two miles north to south, the 14 square miles of land area include 30 cays and probably the best collection of island names in the Atlantic—Devil's Cay, Frazer's Hog Cay, and Fish, Cat, Crab, Cockroach, Bird, Goat, Whale, and Little Whale Cays. These names don't reveal anything about the islands, thus, Frozen Cay is a misnomer.

Great Harbour Cay is located at the northern end of the chain. It has the largest and one of the finest 18-hole, par-72 golf courses in all the Bahamas. At the southern end lies Chub Cay with some of the finest diving in all the Bahamas.

For 25 years, the Chub Cay Club was a private club for the very wealthy. In the past few years, it has been open to the public and, with a full diving facility, has in a short time become one of the top dive locations in the Bahamas.

Still attempting to remain a secret, there are no commercial flights available to the Berry Islands, but regular charter service is available from Nassau, Miami, and Fort Lauderdale.

The dive resort has always geared itself toward photographers. Several schools of underwater photography have chosen Chub Cay as a site to conduct classes. Camera rentals are available and the resort has in-house E-6 film processing available.

A school of silversides parts as a diver descends amongst them. Photo: Keith Ibsen. ▶

Typical Depth Range:	10–20 feet (3–6 meters)
Typical Current Conditions:	None
Expertise Required:	Novice and snorkeling
Access:	Boat

Mama Rhoda Rock is perhaps the most popular dive site in the Berry Islands. The Bahamian government recently added the reef area that includes the Mama Rhoda Rock dive site to the Bahamian National Trust, so the area is protected. All the marine life is safe from hunters, collectors, and poachers to ensure that the area will be maintained as it is today.

No one knows exactly why plant or animal life flourishes in one area and not in another area with similar characteristics. Mama Rhoda Rock is such an area, and it is the shallow-water hard corals that distinguish this area from the others.

An arrow crab, plucked from its hiding place in a lace basket sponge, remains still while its portrait is taken.

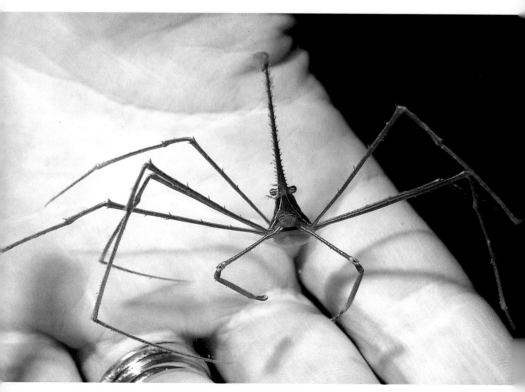

There is literally a forest of elkhorn and staghorn coral. They are so thick in some areas that divers can't fit between the arms of the coral; they can only skirt the area and watch the fish that swim about.

Common to all shallow, coral-encrusted reefs are the reef fish. This is where fish stories are created. There are schools of yellow trumpetfish, a species usually alone when on the reef. But here, they are joined by French grunts, tangs, and snappers. All the small tropicals seem to thrive on the fish campus.

This site is very popular with snorkelers. The air over this site will be filled with snorkel-talk—squeals of excitement that snorkelers yell into their mouthpieces thinking they can be heard underwater. They do not realize that all the sound goes out the snorkel and across the water, entertaining those waiting on the boat.

Photographers looking for fish as models need not make another dive after this one. With or without scuba, don't miss this dive site.

Rows of sand dollars give evidence of the richness of underwater life throughout the Bahamas. Live sand dollars are abundant in shallow sandy areas offshore of the Family Islands.

Chub Cay Wall   10

Typical Depth Range:	80–110 feet (24–30 meters)
Typical Current Conditions:	None
Expertise Required:	Intermediate
Access:	Boat

Located at the northern end of the Tongue of the Ocean, Chub Cay possesses some of the best wall diving in the Bahamas. The best is surely the dive site known as Chub Cay Wall.

Since it borders the "tongue," this wall often gives the diver a glimpse similar to diving in the open ocean. Large pelagic fish, marlin, tuna, and an occasional large shark are not uncommon on this dive.

Schools of horse-eye jacks, crevalle jacks, and large barracuda are regularly seen either alone or in schools. There have been sightings of eagle rays gliding in formation along the wall and "buzzing" groups of divers. This is a treat, especially if you have a camera ready.

This site has a regular collection of smaller fish that are willing to pose for cameras or allow divers to follow them around while they show off their reef. And if you aren't familiar with spider crabs, you're sure to see them on this dive.

The wall is a series of overhangs; each niche is a dive site in its own right. Large black coral bushes adorn the reef at these depths and are highlighted in the clear water.

Gorgonian fingers reach from the depths of the Chub Cay Wall toward the sunlit surface 100 feet (30 meters) above. Gorgonians are common at all depths in the Bahamas.

◄ Brightly colored squirrelfish, like their namesakes on land, dart in and out of hiding places in the reef to examine divers who trespass their coral forests.

6

Diving Bimini

Bimini is usually the first site in the Bahamas seen by visitors. Located only 42 miles (67.5 kilometers) east of Miami, the directional antenna used by aircraft is on Bimini and most planes fly over this small island en route to distant islands.

Since it is so close to the U.S. mainland, and so small—the main island is only 7 miles (11.2 kilometers) by 700 feet (213 meters)—this part of paradise is often bypassed for more distant locations.

Alice Town on North Bimini is the main city on the group of small islands consisting of North Bimini, South Bimini, Cat Cay, and Gun Cay, all of which are referred to as Bimini. The population of Alice Town varies, depending on which fishing tournament is being held at the time. Called the capitol of big game fishing, and often referred to as the Wimbledon of the fishing world, this group of islands alongside the Gulf Stream boasts many fishing records.

Bimini was made famous by Ernest Hemingway who lived, played, and fished here; there is still a Hemingway "air" about the place. Many of the bars claim they were "Papa's" hangout. Every day, someone claims to be the reincarnation of that not-so-long-ago resident of this "island in the stream."

This popular fishing spot with its proximity to the mainland has recently become an important dive spot. Bimini has the Gulf Stream brushing its shores and, therefore, perhaps the best visibility of any island in the Bahamas chain. The reefs around Bimini have become regular stops for live-aboard dive boats.

The cement-hulled Sapona *was once used as a target by Navy pilots. Scattered wreckage and outstanding coral and sponge growth make this one of the finest dive sites in the islands. Photo: Keith Ibsen.* ▶

Typical Depth Range:	15–20 feet (5–6 meters)
Typical Current Conditions:	None
Expertise Required:	Novice
Access:	Boat

Diving on the wreck of *Sapona* is like diving into the pages of history. This 300-foot (91-meter), cement-hulled ship was built by Henry Ford to be used as a troop carrier during World War I. After the war, when prohibition was declared and Bimini became a major gateway for rum runners who brought illegal alcohol into the United States, the *Sapona* hull was used to warehouse contraband waiting for shipment into Florida.

Firmly grounded by a hurricane, the fully upright ship became a target for Navy fighter pilot trainees during World War II. Now, long after it should be nothing but history, it has found a place as one of the finest dive sites in the Bahamas.

The sides of the ship are perforated, making it easy for divers to swim in and out of the gigantic wreck. Since it has been aground so long, the coral and sponge growth are well-established and outstanding. Like all wrecks, the fish life on the *Sapona* is incredible. Schools of French grunts and snapper seem eager to share their home with divers. The pufferfish around the *Sapona* are more numerous than at most Bahamian dive sites.

The mature coral growth on the wreck makes this an excellent location for macro and close-up photography. Since the wreck is so shallow and open, the lighting is great for almost any kind of photography.

Typical Depth Range:	130 feet (39 meters)
Typical Current Conditions:	5 knots
Expertise Required:	Advanced
Access:	Boat

There are several "drift" dives available in the Bahamas, but most of them are "cut" dives, which depend on tide flow during tide change. That is not the case on Bimini. The drift dive along the wall here is provided by the Gulf Stream which never rests. This was previously an occasional dive that is now on the list of regular weekly dives.

In near-perfect camouflage, these French grunts swim and sway beneath the protective arms of a stand of elkhorn coral, reflected on the undersurface of the warm Bahamian waters.

Sponges such as this one are resilient yet fragile. A tear in the tissue of the sponge opens it to invasion by other organisms. Divers are cautioned against carelessness that could cause such an injury to the animal.

The wall plunges to more than 2,000 feet (610 meters), but the dive along the wall is controlled by a drift line so divers do not go below 130 feet (39 meters). The dive is very well-planned, and even divers not used to these depths will feel safe. The extreme clarity of the water, brought about by the Gulf Stream, will erase the perception of depth.

Drifting past the wall is like hang gliding in the Grand Canyon. Where the Grand Canyon was forged in barren land, the ocean reef here is just the opposite.

The Gulf Stream, in its constant flow, carries nutrients with it that enrich the area they pass and cause sponges and gorgonian corals to flourish here more than at any other area in this part of the world.

Along with the sponges and corals, the fish life is second to none. It is tempting to bring a camera along to capture the abundance of life here; however, unless you want wide-angle shots that can be panned as you go by, this dive site is best captured in the mind, and it surely will be.

Being past the edge of the wall and into the "Stream," you are likely to see the large pelagic fish—marlin, tuna, or swordfish—that have made this area the fishing capital that it is.

When you get back home, this is the kind of dive that will be talked about on "bench" dives—those second-hand dives where you meet other divers at the local pub, sit on the *bench,* and talk about diving.

Basket sponges are seen throughout the Bahamas. Some types grow to tremendous sizes, and several have been found that would be large enough to allow two or three adults to sit inside. Care should be taken when handling these giants because they are usually fragile.

Guidelines for Protecting Reefs

1. Maintain proper buoyancy control and avoid over-weighting.

2. Use correct weight belt position to stay horizontal, i.e., raise the belt above your waist to elevate your feet and move it toward your hips to lower them.

3. Use the tank position in your backpack as a balance weight, i.e., raise the backpack on the tank to lower your legs and lower the backpack to raise your legs.

4. Watch for buoyancy changes during a dive trip. During the first couple of days, you'll probably breathe a little harder and need a bit more weight than in the last few days.

5. Be careful about buoyancy loss at depth; the deeper you go, the more your wet suit compresses and the more buoyancy you lose.

6. Photographers must be extra careful. Cameras and equipment affect buoyancy. Changing f-stops, framing a subject, and maintaining position for a photo often conspire to prohibit the ideal "no-touch" approach on a reef. So when you must use "holdfasts," choose them intelligently.

7. Avoid full leg kicks when working close to the bottom and when leaving a photo scene. When you inadvertently kick something, stop kicking! Some divers either panic or are totally oblivious when they bump something.

8. When swimming in strong currents, be extra careful about leg kicks and handholds.

9. Secure dangling gauges, computer consoles, and octopus regulators. They are like miniature wrecking balls to a reef.

10. Never drop boat anchors onto a coral reef.

7

Diving Crooked Island and The Acklins

These islands look like a giant seahorse when viewed from the air. Crooked Island, which makes up the head of the horse, was, according to island history, visited by Columbus who named the island Fragrant Island. The name was arrived at, according to Columbus' diary, because of the aroma produced by the native herbs. One of those herbs—cascarilla bark—is today one of the island's chief exports.

Pittstown Point at the northwest tip of the island is the diving center for Crooked Island and the Acklins. A wall surrounds the underwater perimeter of the island on the western and northern side providing excellent wall diving. Pittstown Point is the home of the oldest post office in the Bahamas.

The National Geographic Society has analyzed Columbus' log book with modern techniques and has traced his route under relative conditions. If these findings are accurate, Crooked Island is what Columbus originally named Santa Maria de la Concepcion, his second landfall. What experts do agree on is that Columbus landed on Crooked Island some time during his first voyage in 1492. And whatever the facts are, the island still smells sweet, the people are friendly, and the diving is great!

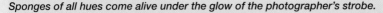

Sponges of all hues come alive under the glow of the photographer's strobe.

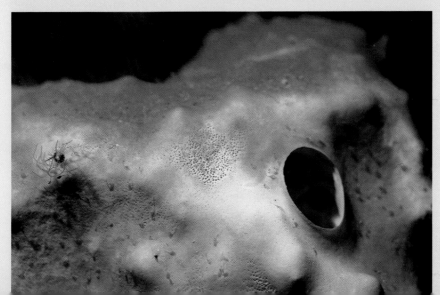

Grandpa Grouper 13

Typical Depth Range:	35–80 feet (11–24 meters)
Typical Current Conditions:	None
Expertise Required:	Intermediate
Access:	Boat

Most of the diving on Crooked Island is wall diving. In some areas, the wall drops off beginning at 35 feet (11 meters); in others, the drop-off does not occur until 80 feet (24 meters). The dive site known as Grandpa Grouper is between these areas, and is named after a pet grouper friendly with divers. "Grandpa," estimated to be a little over 300 pounds (136 kilograms), is more accurately a jewfish.

"Grandpa" is, however, only one of the many large fish seen by divers in this part of the Bahamas. On the edge of the wall, large pelagics are a regular sight along with many varieties of sharks. Turtles are often seen coming through the coral to "check out" the divers.

Crooked Island is not one of the major diving areas; it offers almost virgin diving. Large bushes of black coral in shallow depths are common. On other islands, in more heavily dived areas, the black coral has been destroyed in the shallow depths and divers must go deeper to see it.

Sponges flourish along the edge of the wall with all varieties being represented; some have grown to immense sizes. It is helpful to have a witness or camera when diving near Crooked Island to verify the size of the marine life common to this reef.

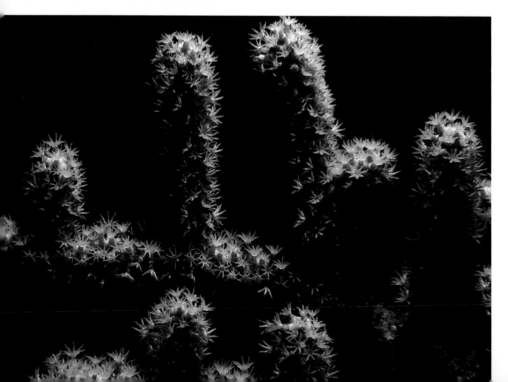

▲ Flaring his gills in a look of aggression, this 15-pound (6.8-kilogram) tiger grouper heads straight for the camera. The white sand on the shallow reefs enhances the natural lighting, making available-light photography possible with even the most basic camera.

◄ Resembling a bush of cholla cactus, these fingers of coral are quite the opposite— soft, smooth, and pliable living animals.

8

Diving Eleuthera

If one of the islands in the Bahamas is the cradle of history for the country, Eleuthera surely is. It is unknown where the first settlers landed, although it is accepted by everyone that towns on Eleuthera were founded and established before Nassau.

In 1648, English Puritans en route from Bermuda shipwrecked off North Eleuthera. All but one of the seventy on board survived; but their ship and all supplies were lost. The captain and a few of the crew sailed to Virginia and borrowed a larger boat and enough supplies to survive. They named their new home Eleuthera after the Greek word *elutheria,* meaning freedom.

The Eleutheran Adventures Company received a grant of 600 English pounds from fellow Puritans in New England. In 1650, as a payback, the settlers on Eleuthera sent ten tons of red dyewood, called brazilleto, to their benefactors to the north. The valuable wood was sold and the money used to support the fledgling new university that today is Harvard.

Settlers left Eleuthera and established Charlestown, which later became Nassau. Dunmore Town on Harbor Island was the capitol of the Bahamas before Nassau. Established in the 1700s, many of the original homes built there are still standing. A church in the center of town was built in 1834 and is still the largest Methodist church in the Bahamas.

Nicknamed the Breadbasket of the Bahamas, the island is 100 miles (161 kilometers) by less than one mile (1.6 kilometers) in some spots. Eleuthera is noted for the many farms and ranches that supply meat, milk, and vegetables to other islands throughout the country.

Eleuthera is probably best known for its "pink sand beach." A three-mile stretch of powder-sand beach on Harbor Island is noted for its pink hue in the bright sun, and mauve coloring during the early and late hours of the day. Originally theorized to have been formed from ground-up conch shells, the "pink" in the sand has recently been found to be small plankton-like animals that flourish in the waters off Harbor Island.

There are three airports serving Eleuthera. A well-maintained road runs the length of the island. Visitors to Spanish Wells and Harbor Island arrive at North Eleuthera airport, take a land taxi to the eastern shore and then a water taxi to the resort. All this adds to the charm of the "Garden Islands."

Typical Depth Range:	50–65 feet (15–20 meters)
Typical Current Conditions:	Strong
Expertise Required:	Intermediate
Access:	Boat

This dive is perhaps the most requested dive on Eleuthera, in spite of the fact that the depth would allow almost an hour underwater, and yet the dive actually lasts no more than 10 to 12 minutes.

If you have ever used the word "excitement" in describing a dive or explaining why you took up scuba diving, you will learn a new meaning for the word on this dive.

Current Cut is a passage between Eleuthera Sound and the open sea that separates North Eleuthera and Current Island. The "cut" is a channel between walls that are approximately 75 yards (69 meters) apart with a depth of 65 feet (20 meters) at the deepest spot.

Divers are dropped off at one end of the cut and picked up at the other end. The direction depends upon the flow of the tide. It takes about 10 to 12 minutes to pass, and a dive usually consists of three passes. During the

Water taxis take visitors from Eleuthera to Harbor Island, one of the first colonial settlements in the Bahamas. Never touched by hurricane damage, many of the buildings on Harbor Island date back to the 1700s.

dive the depth varies between 30 and 60 feet (9 and 18 meters). The current, created by tide change, carries the diver along with it. The diver is in the hands of the current and is as maneuverable as fins and body English will allow. The tide flow, at 6–10 knots, is much stronger than the ability of any swimmer.

Until you gain some expertise, which usually begins about the third pass, the control of the tide flow can send you anywhere. This may result in the diver coming up against some sharp coral, so be sure to wear some protection. A wet suit, bodysuit, or jeans work well.

The visibility isn't as great as at other Bahamas dive sites due to the rush of millions of gallons of water moving through the cut at every tide change.

It's not uncommon to notice a school of jacks riding with you, and larger fish like grouper, barracuda, or stingray often ride the current hoping for a free lunch as some smaller fish are swept up in the flow. Also reported are formations of eagle rays drifting and gliding with the tide between the walls that line the cut.

The Current Cut is a feature dive of dive operators on Harbor Island and Spanish Wells. This dive is the closest a scuba diver will ever come to feeling the sky diver's sensation of free fall.

Schools of silversides, similar to a large cloud, are present on many of the deeper dive sites. Caves and caverns formed by the coral will often house tens of thousands of the small fish. When a diver swims into the cloud, the fish will part and reform around the diver, enveloping him in a silver case.

Typical Depth Range:	15 feet (5 meters)
Typical Current Conditions:	None
Expertise Required:	Novice and snorkeling
Access:	Boat

The famous Train Wreck dive site off the northern tip of Eleuthera Island is one of the most recognized of all dive sites. During the Civil War, the ports of the South were blockaded by Northern ships and trade was almost cut off entirely. The Bahamas became the ports where the Confederacy exchanged cotton and other southern crops for needed war materials. During the mid-1800s, blockade running between the South and the Bahamas became a profitable venture for many.

In 1865, a wooden barge left the dock in North Eleuthera. The barge had several railroad cars on board including a locomotive. It got underway

The blossoms of this beautiful flower bouquet, in delicate pinks and blues, are actually the tentacles of tube worms, extended to capture nutrients.

during a storm, and 10 minutes later sank in 15 feet (5 meters) of water in the center of an area today known as the Devil's Backbone.

This area was the site of several shipwrecks over the years, but none as famous as The Train Wreck. It is an excellent site for beginning divers and snorkelers. Elkhorn corals, so large they rise well above the waterline at low tide, share space with brain coral that are nearly as large and just as impressive. The only remains of the hundred-year-old wreck are a few sets of train wheels.

Fish flourish in this area, as they commonly do at wreck sites. But at the Train Wreck this is probably due to guests who feed these fish, since there is very little left of the wreck to provide habitats. Feeding grouper is common on many dive sites throughout the islands; but here the number and variety of fish that can be hand-fed is remarkable. Blue tangs, triggerfish, and several kinds of angelfish join the tame groupers who beg for food and pose for pictures.

Peacock flounder, a species of left-eye flounder, are abundant here. These brown flounder, covered with bright blue rings, are experts at camouflage, so look closely for them.

Sponges, including the ones used to wash cars back home, are all basically the same. The colorful sponges in the tropical waters are not as soft as the commercial variety, but certainly make more interesting photo subjects. The common commercial variety was a major economic contributor to the Bahamas until the late 1930s when a bacterial infection destroyed 90 percent of the sponge population.

Typical Depth Range:	40–90 feet (12–27 meters)
Typical Current Conditions:	None
Expertise Required:	Novice
Access:	Boat

The range of this dive gives every class of diver from novice to advanced a taste of "wall diving." This site is a mini wall with the ridge at 35–40 feet (11–12 meters) and the bottom at 75–90 feet (23–27 meters).

On the wall, the local divemasters estimate that approximately 90 percent of all species of Atlantic coral are represented, and with the various corals come the life they support. Nudibranchs, flamingo tongues, and lettuce slugs are common sights. Seeing all these animals on one dive is getting to be rare in our modern, crowded dive world.

But the tiny life forms are not the main attraction of this site. The Plateau is home for larger fish, such as an occasional hammerhead and schools of horse-eye jacks, and the fish sizes in between fill this area with wildlife. Before a dive, I asked one of the divemasters, "Are there many fish on this site?" In a word, he said they were "solid"—he was right.

At 80 feet (24 meters), armor-like sheets of plate coral provide nooks and crannies where fish can hide.

The Grotto 17

Typical Depth Range:	45–80 feet (14–24 meters)
Typical Current Conditions:	None to occasionally strong
Expertise Required:	Intermediate
Access:	Boat

There are several classes of divers—not just in their qualifications, but in what they enjoy about the sport of diving. Hunting, treasure, and photography are only some of the aspects that "turn on" a scuba diver. Most divemasters we've met are "turned on" when they discover a new dive site.

Well, this dive site is newly discovered and sure to be a "turn on" for more than just the divemaster who found it. The Grotto has none of the dangers of cave diving but all the thrills. Not really a cave, this large "grotto" nestled in the limestone coral can only be called *exciting.* And it supports all the treats of cave diving: Sleeping sharks are not uncommon, and not only nurse sharks but also a napping reef shark in the 6- to 8-foot (1.5- to 2.5-meter) range are regular features.

Only 30 minutes by boat from the Harbor Island resorts' docks, this is a must-see site. Look for the jewfish that frequents the area; that's a treat worth the ride.

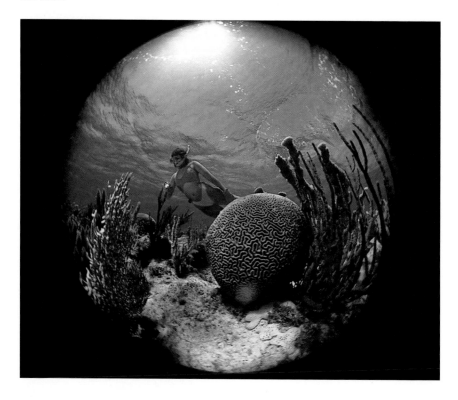

Photography

Both above water and below, subject matter is endless for amateur and professional photographers in the Bahamas. From sunrise to sunset, photography possibilities reinforce the phrase "It's better in the Bahamas."

Throughout the year flowers of all types are in bloom. From the wild orchids in the "bush" to the multicolored hibiscus along the roadsides, the colorful vegetation makes great subject matter or fabulous background settings. Nothing adds to a sunset or sunrise picture like palm trees and calm shorelines. There is always a smiling Bahamian nearby, eager to be remembered in your vacation album. Take an extra shot and send it back to your model and, even if it is ten years before you return, you will still be remembered as the guest who sent back the picture. Underwater, you'll only regret that you can't change lenses or reload film during a dive.

Every dive operation has several dive sites that are favorites because of the fish. On these sites the fish are hand-fed. These same fish (sometimes very large grouper or moray eels) will become a bother trying to get their picture taken after the feeding is over.

The clarity of the water allows good photography, even on the deep dives, using natural light. These waters are excellent for macro and close-up photography because of the variety of subject matter. The subject matter changes from site to site and island to island. Shells, tubeworms, and crustaceans will vary in size and color as well as quantity.

If you have an interest in photography, don't shy away from trying it underwater. Borrow or rent equipment before your Bahamas dive vacation because underwater conditions here are the best! Many resorts and dive operations offer photography courses and carry rental photo equipment. If you're an underwater photographer, you will surely return to the Bahamas.

◄ Photo opportunities are limitless in the azure Bahamian waters. Photo courtesy of Bahamas Ministry of Tourism.

9

Diving Exuma

Three hundred and fifty islands and cays make up the string of islands known as the Exumas. The chain of islands, central in the Bahamas, is about 130 miles (209 kilometers) long and crescent-shaped running north to southeast. The northernmost island is about 35 miles southeast of Nassau. The chain ends on Great Exuma Island, the largest and most populated. It is one of the most beautiful of all the groups of islands in the Bahamas.

Exuma is calm for 51 weeks of the year. The one exception is a week in April when the people of George Town on Great Exuma host the Family Island Regatta. This event tops the Bahamian sporting events calendar. Thousands of Bahamians and visitors watch Bahamian working boats attempt to outsail each other in Elizabeth Harbour off George Town.

During Family Island Regatta week, George Towners, who number less than a thousand, turn their city into a miniature version of New Orleans at Mardi Gras time. This event began in 1954 in an attempt to preserve the wooden boat building skills that make Bahamian fishermen famous.

During the three days of racing, the boats take on as much ballast as they can. The ballast is sand and 18 of the heaviest crew members available, who vigorously compete for money and honors. Top honor is the Prime Minister's Trophy, which is usually presented by the prime minister.

During the evening, after the day's racing, the sailors and visitors continue taking on ballast—in the form of food and drink. When the goombay music starts, and the rum punch begins to flow, George Town comes alive with dancing and celebration throughout the night.

The Exumas are located between Exuma Sound on the east and the Great Bahama Banks on the west. Along the eastern shore, the Bahama National Trust has established 177 square miles (458 square kilometers) of underwater park named the Exuma Cays Land and Sea Park. This area is literally untouched underwater; the diving here is excellent.

Uniquely shaped basket sponges provide hiding spots for small animals. If divers approach with care, the basket sponge will usually reveal a rare visual treat. ▶

Sting Ray Reef   18

Typical Depth Range:	30–50 feet (9–15 meters)
Typical Current Conditions:	None
Expertise Required:	Novice
Access:	Boat

On the outside of Stocking Island, near the edge of Exuma Sound, this dive site is a half-hour boat ride from George Town. A short distance from the site is the Stocking Island drop-off and great wall diving.

Sting Ray Reef is not your normal shallow dive. In addition to the abundant reef fish, there are French grunts, snappers, angels, and tangs. This site, located near the edge of the wall, often hosts large fish who usually make their home in deep water and are seldom seen on shallow sites. Here, however, they are often seen swimming in and out of the coral.

This site was named because it is common to see large stingrays buried in the sand up to their eyes. Turtles are seen regularly, and sometimes large dolphins come by in groups of two or three to check out the divers.

This site is often used as a night diving site. The bottom is covered with both hard and soft coral; there are areas that are covered with different sponges including large tube and basket varieties.

There are always lobsters and crabs tucked in the crannies of the rock and coral. Feather worms and schools of small fish make this an excellent site for close-up and macro photography. Or you might want your camera set up to shoot the dolphins.

Often partially covered with sand, the southern stingray can be hard to spot. By approaching cautiously, a diver can usually get quite close to this member of the shark family. The ray's sharp barb at the base of the tail is used for defense. Photo: Keith Ibsen.

Typical Depth Range:	30–90 feet (9–27 meters)
Typical Current Conditions:	None
Expertise Required:	Intermediate
Access:	Boat

Blue hole diving is mysterious, exciting, and surprising. It's also safe as long as it is conducted within the ability of the diver and without exceeding the planned limits of the dive profile.

Angelfish Blue Hole is a true blue hole—an opening that tunnels back under the island and is subject to the flushing action of the tide change. This dive starts in 30 feet (9 meters) of water. The opening of the hole is 36 to 40 feet (11–12 meters) across and angles off at about 45 degrees to a depth of 90 feet (27 meters). At that point there is a large cavern with tunnels and additional caverns branching off from it. The cavern-like room is the end of the dive. It is the deepest that divers without cave-diver training and proper equipment should go. It is very tempting to explore beyond this area but there is plenty to see and experience without taking any unnecessary risks.

The blue hole's flushing action exchanges millions of gallons of water with every tide change. Also, it moves a tremendous quantity of nutrients with the flow. This rush of nutrients is what makes the dive special. The cavern at the 90-foot (27-meter) depth is a room completely encrusted with

Algae growth covers a stand of once live coral. Thousands of life forms make up the living reef, forming a complete ecosystem.

sponges that have flourished in this rich water. The colors are limitless and breathtaking. You may want to take a light to counteract the color loss that happens at this depth.

This dive site got its name from the assemblage of fish that wait for the free meal that the current flow guarantees. Schools of fish of all kinds will overwhelm the diver. A school of French angels that dive guides and guests have been hand feeding for years are as tame as any fish you will encounter. If you want to photograph these French angels, you'll need someone else to feed them to allow enough distance between camera and fish. The angelfish are only part of the fish population that take up permanent residence on this site. Blue tangs, yellowtails, grunts, snappers, squirrelfish, and armies of sergeant majors are all present. Eagle rays, nurse sharks, green morays, and the resident barracudas often watch the divers as well as the smaller fish.

Exuma is famous for its blue hole diving, with Angelfish Blue Hole as the most popular spot for this particular type of diving.

Bahamian Trivia

The motto of the Bahamas is, "Forward, Upward, Onward, Together." The national flower is the yellow elder, and the national tree is the *Lignum vitae*. The national bird is the flamingo, and the national fish is the blue marlin. The national food dish is conch. Conch is eaten raw, fried, baked, boiled, and barbecued—don't miss trying all of them.

Bahamian independence was declared in 1973, and their Independence Day is July 10. The government is an Independent Commonwealth with a Prime Minister as head of government.

The flag is made up of three stripes: blue on top and bottom and gold in the middle with a black triangle covering the left half of the field of stripes.

The population was estimated in 1994 at 251,000. Most of the inhabitants (75 percent) live in cities. Approximately 136,000 live in or around the capital city of Nassau on New Providence Island.

Covering almost 100,000 square miles of ocean, the land mass is only slightly larger than the state of Connecticut.

The United States is the Bahamas' largest trading partner accounting for 74 percent of Bahamian imports. Seventy percent of the national revenue comes from tourism. Thirty-five percent of all non-government jobs are in the tourist industry.

A spiny lobster hides in a crack in the coral. A nocturnal animal, this fellow will emerge at night and wander freely about the reef in search of food. In the morning, he will retreat to the crevice and wait out another day.

This large-eyed squirrelfish extends his fins to pose for the camera. These fish will grow up to a foot in length. Several species of squirrelfish are common in Bahamian waters.

10

Diving Grand Bahama

Grand Bahama Island is grand indeed. For centuries, when the rest of the Bahamas was collecting its history, the only "grand" thing about this island was its size. Seventy miles (112.6 kilometers) long, Grand Bahama is one of the largest of the 700 islands that make up this island nation.

While history was being made elsewhere, Grand Bahama set idle. On the same latitude as Palm Beach, Florida, and about 60 miles (96.5 kilometers) offshore from the United States, this uninhabited tongue of land with its white beaches and low, sun-drenched profile was, and is, every bit as inviting as any of the Bahamian islands.

Beginning in the late '20s and early '30s, workers were brought to the island to harvest the Southern pine forests for U.S. paper mills. In the early 1950s, Wallace Groves, a manager for one of the lumber camps, considered the Bahamas' proximity to U.S. shores and Grand Bahama's location within the island group and sensed a wind from the future. He proposed a plan to the Bahamian government to develop a section near the center of the island and create a free port and industrial complex.

In 1955, the government went along with the idea and signed the Hawks-bill Creek Agreement. Groves' company, the Grand Bahama Port Authority, was granted 50,000 acres of land with an option on a similarly sized parcel. That same year, an act was passed granting various freedoms from taxation for users of the area through the first half of the 21st century. It was then that the history of Grand Bahama began.

In 1963, the Bahamian government authorized casinos and gambling. That was the real beginning. Today Freeport is the second largest city in the Bahamas. Almost 3,000 hotel rooms are available, and air service by nearly a dozen different airlines keeps this island city alive around the clock.

An elkhorn coral tree spreads its branches toward the surface and the sunlight. These shallow-water corals house plant creatures within their animal cells. They require sunlight for photosynthesis. ▶

Diving in the Freeport area is handled by the Underwater Explorers Society (UNEXSO). For almost a quarter of a century, UNEXSO has been a leader in scuba training and dive operation initiative in the Bahamas.

Dive sites on the western portion of Grand Bahama are on the edge of the Gulf Stream, and the warm, nutrient-rich waters create some of the finest diving in the Bahamas. Visibility greater than 200 feet (61 meters) is not uncommon.

Grand Bahama offers dive travelers the best of all worlds: Diving is superb, after the dive there is everything the big city has to offer, and outside the limits of Freeport and away from the big-city atmosphere, Grand Bahama is every bit as Bahamian as any of the Family Islands.

Typical Depth Range:	70–100 feet (21–30 meters)
Typical Current Conditions:	None
Expertise Required:	Intermediate
Access:	Boat

The Underwater Explorers Society (UNEXSO) has for almost a quarter of a century been the leader in diving initiative on Grand Bahama Island. It's only natural, therefore, that they would be the ones to create the perfect wreck dive for Grand Bahama Island. *Theo's* Wreck, if it were full of treasure, would be that perfect wreck dive. Or maybe the treasure just hasn't been found yet.

The wreck is a steel freighter, 228 feet (69 meters) long, lying on its port side in 100 feet (30 meters) of water. The divers at UNEXSO won't disclose how they were able to place the ship on the perfect spot, but it is so placed that a diver can sit atop the prop or rudder at the 90-foot (27-meter) level and gaze down into the 1,000-foot-deep (305-meter) abyss that lies below the Grand Bahama Ledge.

The wreck is relatively new. It was sunk in 1983, but already colonies of fish have made it home. Clusters of spiny oysters have taken residence inside the hull, and large schools of 13 horse-eye jacks, goatfish, and grunts are ready to pose for photographers. There are also several barracudas that patrol the area looking more threatening than they are. And, as with all wrecks, the schools of small and medium-sized reef fish are present in countless numbers. Since the first edition of this guidebook, a 7- to 8-foot (2-meter) green moray eel named "Fang" has taken up residence and become popular as a photo-opp subject.

With the wreck on the edge of the wall facing the open ocean, there is always the occasional pelagic creature that passes by. Sometimes turtles are seen, and there is a 200-pound (90-kilogram) grouper that has been reported enough times to be believable.

The ship, with its five levels of superstructure, is fully intact; but there are several large holes in the decks and sides that allow divers safe entry and exit to the inner parts of the ship.

Theo's Wreck is a great photo subject and no doubt will be featured in some of the upcoming underwater movies that are filmed in these warm tropical waters.

◄ *A flat-topped pontoon boat unloads its cargo of visiting divers, eager to explore the Bahamian reefs.*

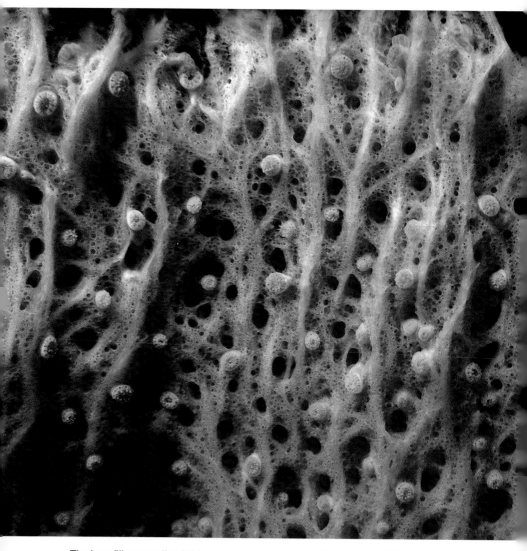

The lace filigree walls of this ocean sponge are actually a colony of thousands of small animals which filter nutrients from the surrounding water.

Resembling an alien landscape, the surface of this sponge demonstrates one of the many secrets and sights awaiting visitors to the living reef. ▶

Typical Depth Range:	45 feet (14 meters)
Typical Current Conditions:	None
Expertise Required:	Novice
Access:	Boat

In the first edition of this book, we featured a dive named Hydro Lab. Well, Shark Junction is the same location but times have changed. Some of the Hydro Lab equipment is still there, but some new residents have moved into the neighborhood. Regularly on this site, eight to ten Caribbean reef sharks, ranging in size from 3 to 9 feet (1 to 3 meters), can be seen.

The sharks keep their distance, and this dive is rated for all divers from novice on up. The divemasters do keep the maximum number on the dive to 16, so there is some control.

Only ten minutes from the dock, this site boasts an abundant number of fish of all kinds. Two friends are a very large black grouper named Notch and a Nassau grouper named Sprout. You'll know as soon as you see them why they are so named.

The old recompression chamber from Hydro Lab has been covered by enough coral now that it looks like some kind of monument. And indeed it is—a monument to diving days gone by.

Pillar Castle 22

Typical Depth Range:	15–20 feet (5–6 meters)
Typical Current Conditions:	None
Expertise Required:	Novice and snorkeling
Access:	Boat

In the center of this dive site stands pillar coral that resembles a castle. Near this castle is a forest of elkhorn coral. Throughout this storybook setting, the fish are abundant. The nooks and crannies in the rocky bottom between the stands of coral are filled with bottom life that includes crabs, lobsters, feather worms, urchins, brittle stars, and spaghetti worms.

This is a perfect site for novice scuba divers and snorkelers alike. It is an outstanding dive for photographing fish and macro subjects. Several small eels live on the rocky bottom. Small rays scurry ahead of the divers and bury themselves in the sand. Small nurse sharks sleep in the shade of coral outcroppings and rock ledges.

The bright shallow-water corals and vivid fish provide an excellent location for natural-light photography. Since it is shallow, there is no color lost.

A diver joins fish amid a colony of pillar coral. Photo courtesy of Bahamas Ministry of Tourism.

Typical Depth Range:	45 feet (14 meters)
Typical Current Conditions:	None
Expertise Required:	Novice and above
Access:	Boat

This dive site is not so much a specific spot amongst the coral; in fact, the bottom is flat sand with small scattered coral. Divers returning from this dive surely would fail any questions asked about the bottom or coral. Yet this dive is the flagship dive of UNEXSO. Once the divers board the dive boat, two adult dolphins swim alongside as the divers load up. Then the dolphins follow the dive boat to the site.

Once the divers are in the water, the dolphins become part of the team. The divers are interactive with these large animals and get a chance to feed them, and now and then divers let the dolphins tow them around. Once someone tries it, the dolphins have a full-time job giving everyone a ride. UNEXSO sends a photographer on the dive, and when you get back there is a video available of you and the dolphins.

The dive is restricted to 12 divers to provide a more intimate interaction between dolphin and diver. Dolphins are known to have personalities of their own, so you'll have to try this dive again—because there are five animals who share the duty, the next dive could be a whole new experience.

Sea stars can be found throughout Bahamian waters. Commonly referred to as starfish, they obviously are not in the fish family. Although some sea stars are considered detrimental, collectively the various species contribute to the makeup of the living reef.

Costumes, three or more times the size of a man, colorfully portray the theme of the Junkanoo parade. Each costume must be entirely supported by one individual.

Junkanoo

Throughout the world, different cultures celebrate the end of one year and the beginning of another in different ways. In China it's fireworks, in Thailand they throw water, in America they sing Auld Lang Syne and watch a ball drop from atop a high building in Times Square in New York City.

In the Bahamas they celebrate with Junkanoo: a tradition brought by slaves from Africa to many parts of the New World. Today Junkanoo survives only in the Bahamas.

The event is celebrated twice—at the end of the old year and the beginning of the new year. The first celebration is on Boxing Day—an English holiday celebrated on the first weekday after Christmas. Originally this was the day that Christmas boxes or gifts were given to servants, workers, letter carriers, etc. The second celebration is on New Year's Day, January 1st.

On these two days, Bahamians parade in large, colorful, papier-mâché and crepe paper costumes. The costumes resemble fish, fruit, parts of the country, or parts of the world. A costume may be the whole world in the form of a giant globe. The only requirement for competition is that the person inside the costume must support the entire costume during the parade.

The parade begins in the middle of the night so the marchers in the heavy, hot suits don't have the warm Bahamian sun to add to their load. It continues until sunrise.

The big celebration is in Nassau, where a square of city blocks are closed to traffic and the parade continuously circles the route until the sun rises.

Most of the Family Islands have a similar celebration. Usually a parade is started in the middle of the night with a "Junkanoo band." The band's instruments include goatskin drums, cow bells, and whistles. Sometimes, newspapers substitute for the crepe paper. Visitors are always encouraged to join in.

In Nassau, where prizes are given for the most elaborate costumes, the competitors are not allowed to use the same costumes on New Year's Day as they used on Boxing Day.

11

Diving Long Island

Long Island is appropriately named. Seventy-six miles (122 kilometers) by only three miles (4.8 kilometers), this string bean-shaped section of land at the southern end of the Bahamas chain is another of Columbus' stopping points. It was here that he first saw natives using what we now call hammocks.

Several towns are scattered the length of the island. The largest settled area is near the Stella Maris Resort at the northern part; this million-dollar facility has become the focal point of the island. It is here that the largest airport is located and where the mail boat "puts in."

Long Island is usually a few degrees warmer than the other Family Islands, especially in the winter months. In summer, the trade winds act as nature's air conditioner and maintain the cool temperatures.

Grouper Valleys 24

Typical Depth Range: 50–90 feet (15–27 meters)
Typical Current Conditions: None
Expertise Required: Intermediate
Access: Boat

The coral reefs throughout the Bahamas' waters have a tendency to spoil divers in a hurry. In some areas designated as deep, the clarity of the water shows the bottom so well that actual depth is deceiving, as proven by this dive site on Long Island.

Without a large amount of coral to break up the scenery, this dive gives the diver the feeling of being in open water like no other site. The sensation of "blue water" is definitely part of this dive and is enhanced by the fish life that makes this area famous.

If large grouper have conventions, this must be the spot. Channel-like runners lead out from the land to the sandy bottom. The large fish hide themselves in these trenches, yet some of these fish are so large, they can't be hidden.

Large jewfish, estimated to weigh up to 700 pounds, are regular inhabitants. The larger grouper can often be seen swimming in unison with sharks of equal size. Schools of deepwater fish are frequently seen cruising through the area.

This site is on the north end of Long Island and is a popular dive site for guests at Stella Maris Inn. The boat ride from the marina takes from one-and-a-half to two hours. Guests are usually driven in a car or shuttle to the area and then boated to the site; this cuts the boat ride to about five minutes. The key description of this dive is "BIG FISH."

Decompression Caution: This site does drop off to more than 200 feet in some places. The drop-off is outside the area where guided dives occur, but caution must be taken. One must not stray and create a time/depth condition that could require decompression. The "blue water," or "open water" feeling on this dive makes it necessary to frequently monitor depth gauges and timers.

◀ *Large Nassau groupers frequent the many trenches that make up the Grouper Valley site. Photo: Keith Ibsen.*

Typical Depth Range:	15–100 feet (5–30 meters)
Typical Current Conditions:	None
Expertise Required:	Novice and snorkeling
Access:	Boat

Flamingo Reef is located on the northwest corner of Long Island. It offers almost every type of diving available in the open ocean. The shallow end of the reef covers an area about one-half mile in length. This spot contains a picture-perfect setting for a shallow reef dive.

Depths average 15 to 30 feet (5–9 meters) and are perfect for snorkelers and novice scuba divers. More advanced divers will find this an excellent location for fish photography as well as close-up and macro settings. All Bahamian reef fish frequent the area, as well as lobsters, crabs, shrimp, and a wealth of shellfish. Flamingo tongues are scattered on the sea fans, hence the name of the area. Moray eels and nudibranchs appear to pose for pictures. The sandy areas between the brain coral heads are often a hiding place for sand rays or skates.

For the more advanced diver, the MV *Comberbach* lies in 100 feet (30 meters) of water three minutes off the shallow end of Flamingo Reef. The one-hundred-foot-long (30-meter) steel ship is intact and setting upright on its keel. Built in 1940, the ship hauled cargo for 45 years. Small corals have started to accumulate on it, and many big groupers have begun calling it home. The area around the ship is made up of a great coral reef. Drop-offs of 40 feet (12 meters) are found next to the ship. The ship has not been stripped and, with the clear water, provides a great setting for wide-angle photography.

The distinct markings of this flamingo tongue cowrie are not on the shell but on a thin membrane that spreads out over the shell as protection against encrusting elements in the water. When endangered, the cowrie pulls this mantle back into its shell, leaving a smooth, cream-colored shell with no markings.

Typical Depth Range:	20–30 feet (6–9 meters)
Typical Current Conditions:	None
Expertise Required:	Intermediate
Access:	Boat

The Shark Reef dive at Stella Maris Resort is not only the most popular dive on this island, but perhaps the most well-known of all regular dive sites in the Bahamas. Shark Reef is 30 to 45 minutes away from the resort by boat. The divemasters have been feeding the sharks on this site for years, and there has never been a single instance of injury to divers.

The sharks will be waiting when you anchor above the site; divers can see them swimming below after entering the water. After the guests are seated against the coral backdrop, the dive guides will break out dinner and begin to feed the 6 to 15 sharks that frequent the area.

The types of sharks vary from day to day. Black- and gray-tipped reef sharks, bull sharks, and occasionally a hammerhead are regular inhabitants. A tame nurse shark has often proved to be friendlier than most and might hang around for some petting after the feeding. In addition to the sharks, the reef is home to several rays and a school of horse-eye jacks. Barracuda are sometimes seen; the sharks are always present.

The bottom in the area where the sharks are fed is flat sand. The reef behind the area sports coral and sponges. This is a perfect spot to capture rare close-up photographs of sharks in the wild.

There is minimal risk on this dive; however, the mere thought of being close to sharks may be upsetting for some divers. For this reason, divers should understand the scope of the dive and be prepared for what will happen.

Be sure to save a full page in your logbook to record this dive.

Under artificial light, the feather-fine fronds of a black coral branch take on an autumn orange hue. When viewed in available light, the black coral colonies resemble the delicate green branches of a fir tree.

Sharks and Divers

Viewing large animals underwater is a treasured experience for divers. Seeing sharks has to top the list of memorable sights. Perhaps one of the reasons shark sightings are so rare is because sharks are actually more leery of divers than divers are of them.

The sharks in the waters of the Bahamas are skittish. They will usually leave an area as soon as divers enter the water. Occasionally, one might stay around but seldom will it come close unless it's brought in by chumming. Sharks are basically scavengers and only seek out food that they will not have to work hard to get. Spearfishermen should not trail stringers of dead fish that might attract sharks (spearfishing is not allowed in most popular diving spots).

There is no cause for alarm when seeing sharks. If divers can get close enough to photograph them, it is considered an especially lucky dive.

An oceanic whitetip shark cruises in the clear deep waters of the Atlantic. Sharks rarely venture into the shallow areas frequented by divers, and are more timid than threatening. Photo: Timothy Turnbull.

Typical Depth Range:	15–90 feet (5–27 meters) plus
Typical Current Conditions:	Mild south to north
Expertise Required:	Intermediate
Access:	Boat

"Concepcion" was the name Columbus gave to the second island he visited on his first voyage in 1492, but the present Bahamian island of Conception was never considered to be this original landmark. When the time came to map the area and assign names, the island that was considered to be Columbus' second landfall already had a name, so the label Conception was given to its present land mass. Contrary to its name, this small dot in the ocean is actually an island "beyond conception."

Small, uninhabited, and out-of-the-way, this is surely the deserted island every adventurer has used to fuel his dreams. Diving here has always been accessible only to boaters cruising between the "Virgins" and Florida. Although our time at Conception was limited, we spent two days anchored in West Bay on the northwest corner of the island. The beach was so perfect that we decided this was where all the postcard pictures were taken. A stroll up a small inlet supplied us with all the conch we needed for lunch.

Formerly restricted to divers in their own boats, Conception is now dived regularly by Stella Maris Inn guests on Long Island. The trip can take from two to four hours depending on the boat, so this is usually an all-day trip. Occasionally, operators make an over-nighter of this dive and include some night diving on the shallow reef heads.

Deep convolutions of the brain coral are the frequent anchorage for Christmas tree worms. Divers should also watch carefully for bristle worms which blend into the twists and grooves of the brain coral.

At night, coral polyps display a completely different picture than during the day. This coral resembles an explosion of tiny lights similar to sparklers.

There is a wall at Conception with the edge in about 90 feet (27 meters) of water. The coral formations start at about 15 feet (5 meters), and all the area in between is good diving.

The coral here is unhampered by anchoring and careless divers. Black coral can be seen as shallow as 60 feet (18 meters), a rare treat seldom enjoyed in heavily dived waters.

Conception has been designated by the Bahamian Government as a park reserve and turtle breeding island. Because of this and the scarcity of divers, animal life is abundant. In the shallows, we saw purple fans with flamingo tongues so plentiful that they looked like berry bushes.

Cruising along the wall at a depth of 80 feet (24 meters), we looked out into the blue water just as two bull sharks were cruising about seventy feet away. The dive guides who accompany the trips to this island report regular sightings of schools of nurse sharks.

The coral formations along the edge of the wall provide endless caverns, tunnels, and channels. Several large coral formations, about 100 by 200 yards (91 by 183 meters), are perched on the edge of the wall like castles towering over the depths. The wall falls off to thousands of feet, creating a rich pure blue color with no visible end.

Seven miles (11.3 kilometers) north on Southhampton Reef in 25 feet (8 meters) of water, there lies the wreckage of an eighty-year-old, 10,000-ton-class freighter. It is broken up, covers an area about 100 by 300 yards (91 by 274 meters), and makes an interesting dive for photography.

Students in a "night school" pick up the beam of a diver's headlight as they make their way above the nightlife on the reef. ▶

Night Diving

If you've been longing to experience night diving, the Bahamas is the perfect place to satisfy that interest. If you are already an experienced diver, but have never been on a night dive in the Bahamas, be prepared to experience a new dimension in diving!

Night diving always conjures up the idea of an experience wrapped in mystery. It is a time when strange creatures come out to play or feed.

Many larger fish and sea inhabitants are present in daylight but are seldom seen because they are more afraid of divers than divers are of them. This also applies at night, although some members of the ocean family can only be seen under the cover of darkness.

Coral heads form beautiful undersea gardens of graceful shapes. They are, in fact, millions of living creatures that are hidden in daylight and blossom only in darkness. These rigid formations become flowering colonies drawing nutrients from the sea around them. Shine a light on them and they retreat back into their day mode.

Reef fish who keep their distance in daylight tuck themselves into crannies in the coral formations and sleep until morning. A diver at night can come within inches of these animals, with or without a camera.

In the clear waters of the Bahamas, night diving is often only a darker rendition of a daytime dive. If you happen to night dive under a full moon with no cloud cover, it will often be so bright on shallow dive sites that the coral and other night life cannot be seen.

12

Diving San Salvador

When Columbus set foot on land in the New World in October 1492, the Lucayan Indians who greeted him told him their island was named Guanahani. In thanksgiving, Columbus renamed the island San Salvador in honor of the Order of the Most Holy Savior, the official name of the Brigittine Monks in his hometown of Genoa. The island was later named Watling Island after George Watling who settled there.

At the end of the last century, historians traced the route as it was described in Columbus' diaries and logbooks and decided that Watling Island was where Columbus first set foot in the New World. In 1893, in conjunction with the Columbus Exposition at the Chicago World's Fair, a monument was erected at the exact spot where Columbus was determined to have stepped ashore. In 1925, the name of the island was changed back to the name Columbus chose—San Salvador.

Recently, however, the National Geographic Society has come up with "proof" that Columbus' actual first landing was on an island some 60 nautical miles to the southeast. But if you visit this 14-by-5-mile (22.5 by 8 kilometers) patch of land in the middle of the Atlantic Ocean, don't mention what the National Geographic Society suggests to the San Salvadorians. They firmly believe this was the first landfall in the New World and they will direct you to any or all of the three monuments erected since the turn of the century. One of these places is said to have a footprint of Columbus that was made in soft clay and hardened.

The chief settlement on the island is Cockburn Town. It consists of a church, a store, and The Riding Rock Inn. Riding Rock was closed for several years and divers during that time missed the "better than great" diving for which this island is famous. Riding Rock is back and so is the great diving. It's not known who fed all the tame groupers on the various dive sites while the resort was closed, but they are all still there and waiting to beg a little treat from ready divers.

Nassau grouper can often become tame and will accept a diver's handout. This species of grouper can be distinguished by the dark band running through the eye and five dark bars banding the body. They can attain a length of four feet. Photo: Keith Ibsen. ▶

Typical Depth Range:	40–130 feet (12–40 meters)
Typical Current Conditions:	None
Expertise Required:	Intermediate
Access:	Boat

Throughout the Bahamas there are thousands of dive sites with unusual names. Upon hearing a name, one wonders what a dive site will be like. Often, after a dive, one still wonders how the site got its name.

This dive site by itself is a wonder. Only a five-minute boat ride from the dock, the site is located on the edge of a wall that starts in 45 feet (14 meters) of water. Back from the edge there is a cave, cut perpendicular to the wall, that angles down at 45 degrees and comes out on the face of the wall.

The cave has a large opening on the wall. The top of the opening is in 70 feet (21 meters) of water and the bottom is at 110 feet (34 meters). This is not a cave that requires cave diving experience, but there is that same thrill just before swimming out at the deep end and being over the wall.

Since the dive is on the edge of the wall, there is a good chance of spotting large pelagics, including turtles or rays. The face of the wall in this area is covered with an abundance of purple tube sponges and large plate coral.

Several large grouper have taken up residence in this area. Guests are invited to share in the feeding of these pets, but it is suggested you bring gloves. Groupers frequently can't tell the difference between fish treats and fingers.

Why is this site named Telephone Pole? It's very logical, there's a telephone pole lying next to the opening of the cave.

Typical Depth Range: 40–130 feet (12–39 meters)
Typical Current Conditions: None
Expertise Required: Novice
Access: Boat

Great Cut is a dive the Bahamas has become famous for. It's a wall dive, and wall dives allow divers to dive to any depth they feel comfortable with. Being on the threshold of the open ocean, it's anyone's guess what might show up.

This site boasts schools of Bermuda chubs and midnight parrotfish. Shark sightings are not infrequent, and the cast includes hammerheads, black-tips, and bull sharks.

A little way down the wall, there's a large cavern that all the divers call a cave. Cave diving is more exciting than cavern diving. About 30 by 30 feet (9 meters) this opening, as well as the face of the wall, is filled with black coral. Watched and protected by the divemasters, this treasure is getting harder and harder to find on dives this shallow.

Now and then a turtle is seen, and the extent to which the wildlife is guarded and protected is evident in its abundance. Don't be surprised if you see a 250-pound (113-kilo) jewfish that calls this site home. And the lob-sters at Great Cut are so large that the divemasters call them "lobzillas."

Tube sponges growing closely have become siamese sponges. True members of the animal kingdom, sponges are carnivores. They eat the plankton that passes through the water around them. In the Bahamas, varieties and colors of sponges are limitless.

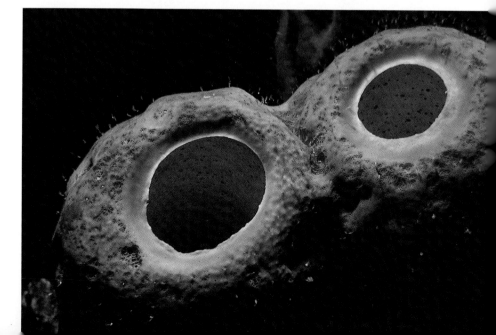

▲ Fan coral or gorgonians are so named because these soft corals with their wood-like stalks contain gorgonin, a protein resembling keratin, the same material other animals use to manufacture fingernails, hair, and hooves.

Small and almost invisible, the banded coral shrimp exists in a symbiotic relationship with larger fishes. ▶

Weather

Weather will not usually pose a problem to divers in the Bahamas. The only weather to worry about is hurricane season between September and November. Many resorts close during this period and take time for annual overhauls and staff vacations.

Rainstorms are usually short-lived, even in the winter months. But because the sand is very coarse, "gin clear" clarity will return within hours after the biggest blow.

Occasionally, you may miss a dive because of weather, but ardent divers can check ahead. There are several resorts that boast they have never missed a diving day due to weather.

13

Safety

Diver Responsibility. Most, if not all, diving you will be doing in the Bahamas will be at a resort or with an established dive operator. Dive operators, divemasters, dive guides, and boat captains are trained in emergency first aid, CPR, and lifesaving in addition to their dive training. They are also well-versed in evacuating injured divers to professional medical facilities.

However, in the final analysis, a diver is responsible for his own welfare. He must avoid hazardous situations and be prepared to handle emergencies calmly.

Part of every dive certification class is devoted to problem management. It is recommended that, before vacationing in an unfamiliar environment, every diver should review this portion of his or her certification manual. It is a good idea to visit a dive shop and look over new manuals and speak to an instructor about new discoveries in diving medicine. You may even want to take a diver rescue class that includes first aid and CPR.

Many Bahamian dive locations include wall diving in their schedule of dives. This will usually involve diving deeper than most divers are accustomed to. Special attention should be paid to the dive tables in order to plan safe dive profiles and avoid decompression sickness.

Chambers. The location and phone numbers for recompression chambers can change frequently. At this writing, there are two chambers available to dive operators in the Bahamas: The Miami Recompression Chamber in Miami, Florida, and the chamber at the Underwater Explorers Society (UNEXSO) in Freeport on Grand Bahama Island.

Miami can be reached through Dade County Fire Rescue, **(305) 596-8576;** U.S. Coast Guard Miami, **(305) 350-5611;** Radio HF 2182; Radio VHF Channel 16; or NOAA (VHF) Channel 9. UNEXSO can be reached at **(809) 373-1244.** These numbers and channels were current at publication. The authors assume no responsibility for these numbers at the time they may be needed.

Rescue service in the Bahamas is also provided by Bahamas Air/Sea Rescue Association (BASRA). There are several different phone numbers for the different islands. Consult the phone directory or ask the operator.

Recompression chamber telephone numbers, and even locations, are subject to change on short notice. Divers should check out these facilities upon arriving in an area where they are unfamiliar with medical and emergency facilities. Phone numbers and important medical information should be kept in waterproof protection in your gear bag. Your "buddy" should know how to reach this information if necessary.

DAN. The Divers Alert Network (DAN) operates a **24-hour emergency number (919) 684-8111** (collect calls accepted if necessary) to provide divers and physicians with medical advice on treating diving injuries. Many emergency room physicians are not aware of the proper treatment of diving injuries. If you find yourself or your buddy in an emergency room with a diving injury, it is highly recommended that you have the physician contact DAN. DAN will have a doctor specializing in diving medicine consult with the emergency room physician. In addition, DAN can give you up-to-date information on the location and telephone number of the nearest recompression chamber accepting sport divers. This varies from time to time, so be sure to check with DAN.

DAN is a publicly supported, not-for-profit membership organization. Membership is $15 a year and includes the DAN Underwater Diving Accident Manual ($4 if purchased separately) describing symptoms and first aid for the major diving related injuries, and the newsletter *Alert Diver* which discusses diving medicine and safety. DAN members are also able to buy a $25 medical insurance policy which covers hospitalization, air ambulance, and recompression chamber treatment for diving injuries. Divers should check with their insurance companies because many will not cover specialized treatment for diving accidents.

DAN's address is: Divers Alert Network, Box 3823, Duke University Medical Center, Durham, NC 27710. Their non-emergency number is (919) 684-2948.

Fire coral is not true coral. It is more correctly a hydrocoral that grows with the coral and has the shape and feel of other stony corals. A beam of light shows the nematocysts that will penetrate the skin if touched and cause a stinging, burning sensation.

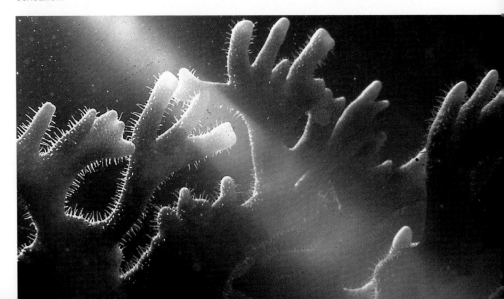

Hazardous Marine Life

Diving in the Bahamas is relatively safe; but as in all sports, carelessness can be hazardous. There are several species of marine life in the waters of the Bahamas that, if abused, are capable of injuring the diver. Most dive operators make it a point to see that guests are forewarned of possible dangers. If you are unaware of what various harmful marine species look like, the divemasters will gladly point them out. The following are some creatures that divers should watch out for.

Barracuda. Barracuda are not aggressive, and they are not as mean as they look. They are fast, however, and will strike at shiny objects that appear to be suitable meals. We once saw a dropped dive knife in shallow water, grabbed by a barracuda before it landed on the bottom.

Bristle Worms. Usually found in shallow water and often under rocks, this animal is as dangerous as it is pretty. It has bristles that cause a sting similar to that of fire coral. Symptoms and treatment are the same as for fire coral.

Coral. With the exception of fire coral, corals are relatively harmless. All corals, however, are covered with a protective mucus. If this should get inside a wound, it could cause infection. Open wounds, where underwater bacteria might have entered, should be cared for and watched. The limestone exoskeleton of the coral polyp colonies that make up the coral reefs is rough and can cause abrasions if bare skin is scraped against it.

Fire Coral. This is not a true coral even though it looks like coral and feels like coral. The secret is, don't feel it. There are tiny nematocysts covering the surface of the fire coral, and if touched these will penetrate the skin. A hot-water soak is the best treatment. The soreness will cease in a short time. A rash may remain after the soreness and itching are gone.

Jellyfish. All jellyfish have some kind of stinging ability. Some stings are so slight that they would go unnoticed unless exposure was to a very sensitive area like the eyes or inside of the mouth. However, it is best to avoid all contact, because touching with the hands might not appear harmful but when the hands come in contact with a more sensitive area, the toxins are likely to rub off and cause irritation. The same hot-water treatment as for fire coral is recommended.

Moray Eels. Moray eels are not known to be aggressive. It is only their bite that is harmful. This usually occurs when feeding is attempted by inexperienced divers unaware of the habits of a particular animal. Morays will not snap at divers unless the divers are teasing them with food. Bites usually transfer bacteria from the animals' mouth and can cause serious infection. It is best to have a doctor examine any bites that cause breaking of the skin.

Rays. Most rays you encounter will be swimming through dive sites and are graceful to look at. Sometimes they will be seen buried in the sand with only their eyes showing, and these are the ones to watch out for. Stingrays are so named for a spike in their tail. If the ray is stepped on or knelt on, it will flip the tail up, driving the spike into its attacker. This spike will cause serious infection and should be treated by a doctor. First aid treatment consists of soaking in water as hot as can be tolerated.

Sea Urchins. Throughout the Bahamas, on all the islands and on all the dive sites, you are likely to encounter the long-spined sea urchins. Their spines are sharp and very brittle. If you merely bump against them without protection, you will get stuck and the spine might break off inside the skin. When this happens, there is usually some soreness that can be relieved by soaking in hot water. After a short time, the soreness will go away, but the purple spot under the skin will remain until the spine works itself out. The best protection is to not touch sea urchins.

Sharks. Seeing a shark while diving in the Bahamas is always a treat because they attempt to disappear whenever divers are present. Sharks have been known to try to steal dead fish hanging on a stringer; but because spearfishing is not allowed on most dive sites, this usually is not a problem. Sleeping nurse sharks are occasionally sighted, and divers can often get quite close to them. Though normally not aggressive, they are unpredictable when shaken from a sound sleep.

Sponges. Some sponges are capable of causing an allergic reaction. Care should be used in handling them and special precautions taken against contact with open wounds.

Appendix: Dive Services

The list below is included as a service to the reader and is as accurate as possible at the time of printing. This list does not constitute an endorsement of these facilities. If operators/owners wish to be included in future reprints/editions, please contact Pisces Books, P.O. Box 2608, Houston, Texas 77252-2608.

Abaco

Brendal's Dive Shop, Ltd.
Green Turtle Cay
Abaco, Bahamas
(800) 780-9941; (809) 365-4411
(809) 367-2572

Dave's Dive Shop and Boat Rentals
Hope Town
Abaco, Bahamas
(809) 366-0029

Dive Abaco, Ltd.
Marsh Harbour
P.O. Box AB 20555
Abaco, Bahamas
(800) 247-5338; (809) 367-2787
Fax (809) 367-2980

Island Marine Dive Shop
Hope Town
P.O. Box G
Abaco, Bahamas
(809) 366-0282
Fax (809) 366-0281

Ocean Exploration Society
Man O War Cay
Abaco, Bahamas
(809) 366-2222; (809) 366-2223

Walker's Cay Undersea Adventures
Walker's Cay
Abaco, Bahamas
(809) 352-5252
Fax (809) 352-3301
U.S. Office:
P.O. Box 21766
Ft. Lauderdale, FL 33315-1766

(800) 327-8150; (305) 462-3400
Fax (305) 462-4100

Andros

Poseidon Dive Bahamas
Lighthouse Yacht Club & Marina
Andros, Bahamas
(809) 368-2308
Fax (809) 368-2300

Small Hope Bay Lodge
Andros Town
c/o P.O. Box N-1131
Nassau, Bahamas
(809) 368-2013; (809) 368-2014
Fax (809) 368-2015
U.S. Office:
P.O. Box 21667
Ft. Lauderdale, FL 33335-1667
(800) 223-6961; (305) 359-8240
Fax (305) 359-8241

Bimini

Bill & Nowdla Keefe's
Bimini Undersea Adventures
Alice Town
North Bimini, Bahamas
(809) 347-3089
Fax (809) 347-3079
U.S. Office:
P.O. Box 21623
Ft. Lauderdale, FL 33335
(800) 348-4644; (305) 462-3400
Fax (305) 462-4100

Scuba Bimini
South Bimini, Bahamas
U.S. Office:
1100 Lee Wagner Blvd., Suite 113
Ft. Lauderdale, FL 33315
(800) 848-4073; (305) 359-2705
Fax (305) 359-2707

Cat Island

Cat Island Dive Center
Hotel Greenwood Inn
Port Howe
Cat Island, Bahamas
Phone/Fax (809) 342-3053

Fernandez Bay Village
Fernandez Bay
Cat Island, Bahamas
(809) 342-3043
Fax (809) 342-3051
U.S. Office:
1507 S. University Dr., Suite A
Plantation, FL 33324
(800) 940-1905; (305) 474-4821
Fax (305) 474-4814

Eleuthera

Romora Bay Club
P.O. Box 146
Harbor Island
Eleuthera, Bahamas
(800) 327-8286; (809) 333-2323
Fax (809) 333-2324

Valentine's Dive Center
P.O. Box 1
Harbor Island
Eleuthera, Bahamas
(800) 383-6480; (809) 333-2080
Fax (809) 333-2135

Exuma

Exuma Fantasea
P.O. Box 29261
George Town
Exuma, Bahamas
(800) 760-0700
Phone/Fax (809) 336-3483

Grand Bahama

Sun Odyssey Divers
77 Silver Palm Court
P.O. Box F-4166
Freeport, Grand Bahama
(809) 373-4014

**Underwater Explorers Society
(UNEXSO)**
P.O. Box F-2433
Freeport, Grand Bahama
(809) 373-1244
Fax (809) 373-8956
U.S. Office:
P.O. Box 5608
Ft. Lauderdale, FL 33310-5608
(800) 992-DIVE; (305) 359-2730
Fax (305) 359-0007

Xanadu Dive Center
P.O. Box F-2846
Freeport, Grand Bahama
(800) 336-0938; (809) 352-5856
Fax (809) 352-4731

Long Island

Stella Maris Inn
P.O. Box SM 105
Stella Maris
Long Island, Bahamas
(809) 336-2106
U.S. Office:
1100 Lee Wagner Blvd., Suite 319
Ft. Lauderdale, FL 33315
(800) 426-0466; (305) 359-8236
Fax (305) 359-8238

San Salvador

Club Med Columbus Isle
Cockburn Town
San Salvador, Bahamas
(809) 331-2000
Fax (809) 331-2222

Riding Rock Inn
Cockburn Town
San Salvador, Bahamas
(809) 332-2631

U.S. Office:
1170 Lee Wagner Blvd., #103
Ft. Lauderdale, FL 33315
(800) 272-1492; (305) 359-8353
Fax (305) 359-8254

Live-aboard Dive Operators

Blackbeard's Cruises
P.O. Box 66-1091
Miami Springs, FL 33266
(800) 327-9600; (305) 888-1226
Fax (305) 884-4214

Bottom Time Adventures, Inc.
P.O. Box 11919
Ft. Lauderdale, FL 33339-1919
(800) 234-8464; (305) 921-7798
Fax (305) 920-5578

Coral Bay Cruises
17 Fort Royal Isle
Fort Lauderdale, FL 33308
(800) 433-7262; (305) 563-1711
Fax (305) 563-1811

Crown Diving Corporation
M/V Crown Islander
2790 North Federal Hwy.
Boca Raton, FL 33431
(800) 245-3467; (407) 394-7450
Fax (407) 368-5715

Nekton Diving Cruises
1057 SE 17th Street, Suite 202
Fort Lauderdale, FL 33316
(305) 463-9324; (305) 463-8938

Out Island Divers—The Bahamas
P.O. Box 350451
Ft. Lauderdale, FL 33335
(800) 241-4591
Phone/Fax (305) 568-9547

Out Island Oceanic
717 SW Coconut Dr.
Ft. Lauderdale, FL 33315
(305) 522-0161

Sea Fever Diving
P.O. Box 39-8276
Miami Beach, FL 33139-0276
(800) 443-3837 (305) 531-3483
Fax (305) 531-3127

Index

Boldface numbers indicate illustrations.